Practical Techniques for Language Teaching

Michael Lewis
Jimmie Hill

Language Teaching Publications
114a Church Rd, Hove, BN3 2EB, England.

Acknowledgements

We are grateful to the following who gave us at least one important idea developed in this book: Rod Bolitho, Professor Hans-Eberhart Piepho, Robert O'Neill, Rolf Ferm, Howard Thomas, Keith Lomas, and Bright and MacGregor.

We are also grateful to the Directors of Studies, particularly Dr Ian Dunlop and Sally Ocklind, of the British Centre, Stockholm, who at different times stimulated our ideas in many ways.

Helen Naysmith and Stephen Whitehouse read and made many helpful comments on the draft manuscripts.

Most importantly we would like to thank the hundreds of teachers at the British Centre, Stockholm, who, having been on training courses run by us, later allowed us to watch them in the classroom.

Finally to the many teachers of English who are not native-speakers whose comments on courses and lectures we have given have provided us with a perspective on the problems of teachers working within State Schools.

It is the discussions with teachers we have trained and seen teaching that are the basis for the suggestions in this book.

The Authors

Michael Lewis taught English in Sweden at all levels from primary school to adult. In 1981 he co-founded LTP. He has lectured on language and methodology in most European countries, Japan, the States and Central America. He is the author of *The English Verb* and co-author of *Business English*. His main current interests lie in the areas of grammar, vocabulary and the development of a semantic syllabus.

Jimmie Hill spent 6 years teaching English in Sweden before returning to the UK to co-found LTP with Michael Lewis. He is the principal author of *Grammar and Practice*, and it is in the theory and practice of grammar that his main interest lies. He is a regular speaker at conferences throughout Europe.

ISBN 0 906717 55 8

Reprinted 1986, 1988, 1990.
New, revised edition, 1992
Reprinted 1995, 1997

Printed in England by Commercial Colour Press Plc, London E7.

Introduction

to the Revised Edition

This book is not theoretical. It is a collection of practical ideas and techniques which you can use immediately to make your own teaching more effective, and more enjoyable for yourself and your students. The book is not based on a method or an approach. We do not believe that there is one way of teaching well. All the suggestions are based on our experience of teachers teaching. Ideas are included because we have seen that they work for a wide range of teachers in many different situations.

Teaching situations are different. You may, for example, have to prepare students for a particular examination so that some time must be spent on examination techniques. All teachers complain that they do not have enough time to do all the things they would like to do. Some compromises between what you would like to do, what your students need, and the requirements of the situation, are inevitable.

In these circumstances there are two guiding principles which should influence your decisions: that language teaching is only an aid to language learning, and that it is those things which help the students to improve which are of particular importance; and secondly that language is first and foremost communication. Those activities which mean students can use the language, and communicate better, are to be encouraged at the expense of activities which will only mean that students "know" the language.

The first two chapters of the book do provide a more general framework for the specific tips which follow. Even these general principles, however, are practical rather than theoretical. You are encouraged not only to read the tips, but to try the ideas they suggest. We hope most will work for you, but some may not, and some will need to be modified for you and your situation.

The book is essentially one of techniques, applicable to different situations and also to different material. Any selection of textbook materials we could make would be in danger of being situation-specific, or based on assumptions about text-books which are widely available at the moment of writing. We believe initial teacher training courses should include an element which shows students how to develop lesson plans round published materials, but in our experience course tutors almost always prefer to use contemporary or local materials in developing these lesson plans. For this reason, we have not included a chapter on specific materials.

In revising this book for its second edition, we consulted many course tutors, and others with experience in the teacher training field. We were delighted to discover that they were happy with the existing text. The main change in the new edition, therefore, is the addition of points which we felt deserved more emphasis. In one or two cases — specifically increased emphasis on receptive skills and collocation — the re-emphasis marks the development in our own thinking since the first edition appeared.

Few teachers, however long they have been teaching, are doing things as well as they possibly could. There is almost always an opportunity for new ideas, attitudes and techniques. We hope this book will encourage readers to try any ideas which are new, and so to develop their teaching, and in turn their students' learning.

Michael Lewis, Jimmie Hill, Hove 1992.

Contents

22. Divide the blackboard.
23. Use the overhead projector to control what students see.
24. Machinery will not solve all your problems.
25. Expand, don't clutter.

4. Preparation 55
1. Prepare yourself.
2. Courses and lessons need an overall structure.
3. Don't let the book dictate.
4. Do not prepare too much or too rigidly.
5. Preparation must be concrete.
6. Aids are only aids if they help.
7. Never ignore the practical difficulties.
8. A good lesson has a beginning, a middle and an end.

5. Techniques — Listening 61
1. Listening can be divided into sub-skills.
2. Direct students' listening, particularly if it is taped.
3. Listening to a tape is difficult.
4. Let students hear "the real thing" from early in their course.
5. Make sure students can hear the difference between similar sounds.
6. Use a variety of 'listen and respond' activities.

6. Techniques — Speechwork 65
1. Do not distort when giving a model.
2. The model must remain the same.
3. Use choral pronunciation.
4. Conduct choral pronunciation decisively.
5. Move around the room when doing choral pronunciation.
6. Keep your language to a minimum in pronunciation practices.
7. Vary your criterion of "good" in pronunciation practice.
8. Articulation is an important first step in practice.
9. It is helpful to do articulation practices more than once.
10. Bring variety to 'say after me'.
11. Something which is not a real word sometimes helps.
12. There is no such thing as the 'c-h sound'.
13. The main criteria for pronunciation are consistency and intelligibility.
14. Teach intonation by back-chaining.
15. Don't explain intonation, demonstrate.
16. Show stress, pitch and intonation visually.
17. Refer to stress and intonation even when not specifically teaching it.

7. Techniques — Structure 75
1. Encourage students to see patterns.
2. Good rules can help students.
3. Understanding involves example, explanation, and practice.
4. Terminology can help or hinder.
5. Filling in a fill-in exercise is not enough.
6. Students need to practise form as well as use.
7. There is a place for oral and written practices.
8. Use 'gimmicks' to combat popular mistakes.
9. Use beehives with large classes.
10. Most language games are structure practices.
11. Free situations are important.
12. Grammar can be fun.
13. Grammar is a receptive skill, too.
14. Teach word grammar as well as sentence grammar.

8. Techniques — Correction 89
1. Mistakes are a natural part of the learning process.

2. Give students the chance to correct themselves.
3. Involve the class.
4. Isolate the problem.
5. The student must use the correct language.
6. There are many kinds of mistakes.
7. Correcting register and appropriacy needs tact.
8. Correct promptly for accuracy, afterwards for fluency.
9. Don't over-correct.
10. Reformulation is often better than correction.
11. Use a code to correct written work.
12. Use class discussion as a basic method of correcting written work.

9. Techniques — Vocabulary 97

1. A 'vocabulary' item can be more than one word.
2. Do not discuss the structure of lexical items.
3. There is a difference between active and passive vocabulary.
4. Explain difference of meaning, not meaning.
5. Words are often best taught in groups.
6. Vary the way you explain.
7. Words can link grammatically as well as thematically.
8. Record words together which occur together.

10. Techniques — Texts 105

1. Different texts have different uses.
2. Too many new words make a text impossible.
3. Nothing is 'interesting' if you can't do it.
4. Use pre-activities to focus students' attention.
5. Distinguish between intensive and extensive reading.
6. Do not ask students to read aloud unseen.
7. Vary the method of reading.
8. Use short questions during intensive reading.
9. Don't ask "What does ... mean?", use definition questions.
10. Students cannot use what they cannot say.
11. 'Difficult' words are not the same as long words.
12. 'Correction questions' prompt student language.
13. Not all comprehension questions check understanding.
14. Use comprehension and conversation questions together.
15. If you read a dialogue, distinguish the two speakers clearly.

11. Techniques — Conversation 117

1. Exploit opportunities for short spontaneous conversations.
2. Don't flog a dead horse.
3. Encourage contributions without interfering.
4. Conversation does not need to be about serious issues.
5. Provocative statements are often better than questions.
6. Problem solving is often an excellent basis for 'conversation'.
7. Encourage active listening.

12. Some misunderstood language points 123

1. Some/any
2. 'The Future'
3. Continuous forms
4. Go-went-gone
5. Countable and uncountable nouns
6. Can/could
7. Must/have to
8. Tags
9. Auxiliaries
10. (do) as the dummy auxiliary

Chapter 1

Basic Principles 1 — Student and Teacher

Before you read this chapter think about each of the following statements.
Mark each statement

✔ if you *agree*.
X if you *disagree*.
? if you are *undecided*.

1. Lessons should be planned and timed carefully.	
2. Sometimes the textbook stops you teaching well.	
3. Language teaching is partly about teaching students how to learn a language.	
4. If students have difficulty it's usually best for the teacher to explain and move on.	
5. The teacher should not be talking for more than 20% of the lesson time.	
6. English is a difficult, illogical language.	
7. I teach each unit of the book in the same way.	
8. I never sit down during my lessons.	
9. I always explain what I'm going to do before I do it.	
10. I don't worry if I don't follow my lesson plan, providing the students enjoy it.	

After you have read the chapter do the same thing. Has reading the chapter clarified your ideas?
Have you changed your ideas?

Basic Principles 1
Student and Teacher

1. Learning is more important than teaching

The conscientious teacher is concerned to teach well. You would not be reading this book unless your intention was to improve your own teaching and a knowledge of theory and technique can help to make you more effective and more efficient. The single most important factor to remember, however, is that teaching is not the terminal objective of what happens in the classroom. In the end, it is changes in the students' behaviour upon which success and failure depend.

The ultimate test of "a good lesson" is not how the teacher performed but whether the students learned. Teachers who are constantly pre-occupied by their own role — what they should be doing, and what their students think of them — are making a serious mistake. The most important role of the teacher is that of catalyst — they help to make things happen, but the purpose is activating the students.

Some teachers have taught the same lessons in the same way for years out of laziness or inflexibility; other teachers make a more subtle mistake — they constantly look for "the method". Such teachers believe that there is 'a best' way of doing something and, having found the method they consider best, they follow it strictly and carefully. We do not believe that such a method exists. Language is complex, and language teaching is correspondingly complex. It is difficult to make *any* statement which is *always* true about language teaching. Different situations call for different materials, different methods, different activities, and different strategies. The main principle for teachers to remember, however, in deciding on the suitability of an approach or method is whether it will be helpful to their particular students in that class. Will it help the students to achieve their objectives? If it does that, the teacher will also have succeeded.

Although it is not always possible for teachers working within the state system to follow this principle completely, it is clear that if the syllabus, book, or teacher are more important than the students, something serious is wrong.

2. Teach the students, not the book

Few teachers have the time or opportunity to design their own courses. In the majority of cases a basic textbook is chosen and it is this which provides the practical classroom syllabus. Inevitably, teachers tend to follow the book, deciding in advance how long they can spend on each unit so that they will finish the book in a certain time. But the object of the course is to teach the students, not finish the book!

It may be necessary to prepare additional practices on particular points; it may be necessary to go back and study again a unit which has caused particular difficulties and, most important of all, it may be necessary to abandon the day's lesson plan because students raise difficulties which neither the teacher nor the book has foreseen. The principle is that if, at any point during the lesson, the teacher's pre-arranged plan and the students' needs are in conflict, it is the students' needs which should have priority.

3. Involve students in the learning process

Some foreign language students, particularly adults, are learning the language for very specific reasons; others, particularly those learning in a State school system, are doing English because it is part of the system. In all cases, however, students are more likely to enjoy the subject, and to succeed at it, if they are involved in the learning process and, as far as possible, have a chance to influence what happens, and how it happens.

It is almost invariably a good idea to begin a new course by discussing with students why they are studying English, what uses they see for the English they learn, and something of their expectations of what they expect to happen in the classroom. It also helps to discuss what students expect to enjoy, and not enjoy.

The discussion should be as practical as possible. Teachers can, for example, distribute a list such as the following and ask students:

To tick uses of English which they think are relevant to them personally.

To arrange the items in order of importance (from 1 to 10).

English is useful because:

A. You can talk to lots of new people.

B. You can use English when you are travelling.

C. You can understand films and TV programmes.

D. You can understand pop songs.

E. It helps you to get a good job.

F. You need it if you want to study at university.

G. People do business in English all over the world.

H. You can understand more about the world if you can read English and American magazines and newspapers.

I. It's the international language for most people.

J. You can read English literature in the original language.

During the course it can help to present students with a questionnaire such as the following.

Mark each of these ✔ if you *can* do it in English.
Mark it X if you *can't* do it in English.

Tell somebody a bit about myself.
Talk about my hobbies.
Make a phone call.
Write a short letter to a friend.
Explain to someone that they have made a mistake.
Tell someone politely that I don't believe them.
Explain what kind of food I like, and don't like.
Talk about my favourite sport.
Say five ways life in my country is different from life in Britain.
Talk about politics.
Read a newspaper article.
Disagree strongly but politely with someone else.

Usually such a questionnaire will work better if the teacher has prepared it specially for the class so that it fits well to what the students have studied, and to what they are going to study in the near future.

After the initial discussion it helps if, from time to time during the course, questions as to *why* students are learning, *what* they are learning, and *how* they are learning, are raised again. The last of these is, perhaps, particularly sensitive and worth further discussion.

Teachers are constantly assessing students, while students have little chance to assess teachers. But why should this be so? Teachers would rather give good, effective, and enjoyable lessons than otherwise. Why not allow their 'customers' to help them to do this? It is self-evident that some lessons are more successful than others, and some lesson activities more popular than others. Ten minutes spent occasionally at the end of a lesson asking students if they have enjoyed that particular lesson or not and, more importantly, *why* they have, or have not, can be very rewarding. First, it demonstrates to the students that they are important in the learning process, and that the teacher is interested in them both as language learners and as people. Secondly, the students can tell the teacher what they enjoy and why. In some cases this information may surprise the teacher, but it should help to make the teaching more effective and more enjoyable. There is no need for the teacher to fear the students' assessment. If their comments are taken seriously, students soon realise that they can usefully influence their own lessons. A simple comment such as students asking to work with a different partner on different days in pair work, or to be given a little longer time to complete group work activities, can help. In the same way a general comment — that the course is going too quickly or they don't get enough chance to speak — is, if seen constructively, invaluable in helping the students, which is the teacher's main objective.

Students' motivation will almost always be better if they see the purpose of what they are doing. Although the objective of a particular practice may be clear to the teacher, it is not necessarily clear to the students. Teachers should be prepared to explain to the students what they are doing, and why they are doing it. Some examples may help:

a. Sometimes you will play a tape which the students are to mimic — it will help the students to *speak* English; on other occasions a tape containing language which the students will not know may be used to help students to *listen* better. Unless you have introduced the second tape and made clear that it is a different kind of practice, students will be confused and you can expect howls of protest.

b. Most modern language courses are cyclical — the same language points recur throughout the course. It can easily appear to students that 'we've already done this'. Teachers must be prepared to explain that they are not doing the same thing again, but learning more about how a particular structure is used.

c. Frequently it is helpful to do the same practice more than once in quick succession. This is true, for example, of articulation practices intended only to develop motor skills (see page 69). It is also true of communicative pair work practices where first attempts at the practice are largely diagnostic and the practice is repeated after the teacher has provided some linguistic input. While the usefulness of such repetitions is clear to the teacher, for school students they contrast strongly with what they are used to in other lessons — there is little point in asking students to do the same maths problem twice.

Long explanations of classroom activity should be avoided, but teachers should constantly be alert to the fact that students will work more happily and more effectively if the purpose of the activity is clear to them.

This principle relates not only to whole lessons but to individual activities. If students are going to listen to a tape, or read a text, it helps to tell them in advance what it is about and perhaps some of the important language they will need to understand it. (See page 62 and page 108). If the emphasis lies on language *learning* and not language *teaching*, it is clear that a methodology which is based on teacher knowing everything and 'revealing' things to students, will be inappropriate. Secrets do not help. On the contrary, the teacher's task is to signpost the course, the lesson, and the individual activities, as clearly as possible for the students.

In the same way that preparation helps orientate students, teachers can make the course seem more immediately useful and relevant by helping students to see what they have achieved, and understand what they can do with what they know.

There are only about 200 verbs in English which have irregular past tense forms and about half of those are extremely rare or archaic. There is no short cut to learning them, but you can make it easier for students by telling them explicitly that there are only a certain number and that if, for example, they learn 10 a day for three weeks they will know *all* the English irregular verbs. The information does not make learning the verbs any easier, but it makes the task seem manageable and less inhibiting.

In a similar way it is unexciting but necessary to practise manipulation of the auxiliary:

A I've just bought a new car.   **A** I'm going to Tenerife.
B Oh, have you.   **B** Oh, are you.

Most modern courses re-cycle structures through different functional uses. In this case it helps to remind students that when they can manipulate the auxiliary in this way, they can make interested responses so that they can take part *actively* in a conversation even if their own English means they cannot say very much.

    The principle is simple — the more the students feel involved in the process of learning, the more successful and enjoyable they will find it.

4. Don't tell students what they can tell you

Most language teachers talk too much. Again, it is important to remember that the primary objective of the couse is to improve the students' language, and to present *them* with opportunities for productive practice (or *carefully controlled* listening practice).

    There are many opportunities in a typical lesson for eliciting knowledge and information from the students rather than simply telling them it:

a. If the work of one day is an extension of something from a previous lesson, students should be reminded of the previous lesson, but by the teacher *questioning* the students, not telling. Examples of this are if a continuous story is being read, students should be asked to summarise the story so far, or, if a language point is being re-studied, it should be introduced with questions rather than teacher presentation.

b. After studying a text, instead of explaining words, ask definition questions (see page 111).

c. Make a habit of asking students to contribute alternative language of their own — for example, another phrase which is functionally equivalent, synonyms, or associated vocabulary items. Word roses and word ladders (see page 108) can be helpful in ensuring that the students provide some of the linguistic input for a lesson.

d. Students can also be encouraged to provide some of the content of a lesson using, for example, the positive/negative technique (see page 59).

The student's language may be limited but this does not mean the student is unintelligent. Too often teachers, particularly native teachers, treat students whose linguistic level is low as if they were generally less able. This mistaken assumption can be particularly unfortunate in the case of a well-qualified middle-aged businessman. Such students not unreasonably expect to be treated as intelligent and capable adults and resent materials or teachers that patronise them.

    On a more general level it is not unusual for teachers to explain at length only for a member of the class to say *We've already done that,* or, in the case of a native speaker the explanation is greeted by *We've got the same word in (Spanish)*. Annoying as this may be, teachers bring such difficuties on themselves.

Allowing students to contribute in this way is not just a gimmick. Firstly, it provides students with more opportunities to say something (and keeps the teacher correspondingly quiet!). It also constantly provides the teacher with an idea of the students' previous knowledge and understanding, and reveals misunderstandings which may need to be cleared up before new work is introduced.

The principle is to base your teaching on eliciting rather than instructing. Such an approach reflects accurately the roles of teacher and student in a classroom which emphasises that learning is more important than teaching.

5. Show your reactions to what students say

Part of exploiting real events involves reacting naturally to what students say, both in exercises and in free conversation. Look at this example:

T   So, have you seen "The Sound of Music"?
S1 Yes, but only on television.
T   And what about you?
S2 No, I don't like musicals.
T   Oh, don't you? Have you seen it, S3?
S3 Yes I have — 18 times.
T   Yes, and what about you, S4?

The teacher's response to S2 is good — it is natural and gives the students a chance to notice a typical feature of active listening *(Oh, don't you?)*. The teacher's reaction to S3, however, is a disaster for two important reasons:
a. A teacher could only react so automatically if he or she was not listening. Realising that you are not listening has a strong demotivating effect on students.
b. The teacher missed a wonderful opportunity to demonstrate in a natural context the intonation appropriate to expressing surprise *(18 times! What on earth for?)*.

If you are surprised, shocked, curious, doubtful, etc. make sure you *show* it in your general reaction, in what you say, and in *how* you say it. Encourage other students to show their reactions too. Such reacting develops an important language skill — the active role of the listener in a conversation — and makes both the language and your lessons more alive for students.

6. Students need practice, not you

There are many ways in which it is possible for the teacher to dominate the classroom linguistically in ways which are quite unnecessary. The more the teacher talks, the less opportunity the students have to speak, but it is the students who need the practice!
Teachers should beware of all of the following:
   a. Explaining when they don't need to.

b. Repeating themselves unnecessarily (for example, when asking a question).

c. Answering for students, without waiting long enough.

d. Correcting too much and too quickly.

e. Talking about something which interests them, but not necessarily their students.

f. Talking unnecessarily about the process of the lesson (see page 44).

It is not, however, sufficient for the teacher to avoid unnecessary talk. If the main classroom activity consists of the teacher asking questions which are then answered by individual students, it still means that half of all classroom language is coming from the teacher. Teachers working in state school systems, for example, need to remind themselves frequently of a calculation such as the following — if the students have four 45 minute lessons a week, in a class of 30, there are only 180 minutes available each week to be divided among those students. Even if the class consisted of no reading, pauses for thought, or other activities, but entirely of the teacher asking individual students questions which were answered immediately, the teacher would do 90 minutes talking and each individual student only three minutes. As soon as the practical difficulties are taken into account, this time is greatly reduced and a more realistic estimate of the time spent talking by each individual pupil would be perhaps a minute a week. In those circumstances it is hardly surprising if students' spoken English improves slowly! However much the teacher may be anxious about it, it is essential that techniques are introduced into the classroom to increase the amount of student talking time. Oral work, pair work, and group work are not optional extras — for the students' spoken language to improve, they are essential.

One word of warning is, perhaps, necessary, There is more and more evidence that good *listening* practices have a more important part to play in good language teaching than has sometimes been recognised. A practice, for example, in which students are given two or three questions and then listen to the teacher talking about something can undoubtedly be very useful. It is not necessary that every practice involves lots of "student talking time." The teacher talking as a planned part of the lesson has an important role to play, *providing* the students are listening actively. Teachers should, nonetheless, be conscious of the amount of *unnecessary* talking they do. The general principle is that if the teacher is talking, the students are not getting the practice they need.

7. Don't emphasise difficulties

Learning a foreign language well is difficult. Many students find it difficult to understand conceptual distinctions which do not occur in their own language, and the memory load is high. There is no point in pretending that these difficulties do not exist. As all teachers know, students, particularly in school, do need to be reminded from time to time that there is no short cut to success. Being realistic about difficulties is an important part of the teacher's job.

Unfortunately, teachers too often make the subject seem more difficult than it is through a series of casual remarks, the main effect of which must be to undermine the students' confidence.

Here are some examples:

> *English is a very difficult language.*
> *English is full of irregularities — there are no real rules.*
> *Well, there's the rule, now let's look at the exceptions.*
> *Prepositions are completely illogical.*

Most teachers will admit to having made these, or similar, remarks. They are obviously unhelpful. It is difficult to think of an occasion when it could be helpful to tell students that what they are struggling to understand is in fact really incomprehensible! Teachers need to be realistic about difficulties — it can be helpful, for example, to tell students before they listen to a tape that the voice has a strong accent. If students are doing a listening-for-gist exercise with a lot of language they may not understand, they need to be told of this difficulty in advance. The principle, however, is for the teacher to be *realistic* about difficulties, and to avoid undermining the students' confidence by casual ill-considered remarks.

8. Vary what you do, and how you do it

While there are many helpful ways of approaching language teaching, it is a mistake to believe that 'a method' exists which can guarantee success. Every teacher knows that what works one day with one class, does not necessarily work with a different class, or even on a different day with the same class. A textbook which is appropriate to one situation, is often not suitable for another. One statement which is generally true can, however, be made — if the teacher always does the same things in the same way, the students will be bored!

Each unit of most basic course books is laid out in a similar way. The introduction to the course book, however, usually points out that this is to provide a convenient framework for the teacher, not so that each unit is taught in the same order, using the same method, day after day.

There are many opportunities for variety:

a.   Teach the unit in a different order — in one case use the dialogue for listening comprehension before the students see the text, on another occasion use the taped dialogue as a summary after studying the printed text and doing the exercises.

b.   Use different ways of reading texts: prepared, dramatic reading, silent reading, the teacher reading, listening to the recorded text, etc. (see page 110).

c.   Vary *who* performs the task — you or the students. It is not, for example, necessary for you always to ask the comprehension questions about a text — the students can ask each other questions.

d.   Introduce alternative activities from time to time — games, pair work, group work, problem solving, project work, etc.

e.   Change the seating plan for different activities and, for example, vary where individual students are sitting for pair work so that on different days they are working with different partners.

A word of warning is necessary. Students like to feel secure in the classroom and they want to know what is going on. Students will be disconcerted if you chop and change in a random fashion. The principle is to have a *constant framework* within which there is a *variety of pace* and a *variety of activity.*

9. Select!

Teachers never complain that they have too much time on a course. The complaint is always in the other direction — *If I had more time I could do...* Within the limits of any course — whether it is a two-week intensive course or a course lasting the whole of the student's school career — the target cannot realistically be a complete knowledge of English. In every case selections have to be made of the language to be presented, the skills to be learned, etc. Certain selections, such as general syllabus design and choice of textbook may, on many occasions, be outside the teacher's control. Even so, the individual teacher is constantly faced with selections. The most dangerous "selection" of all is an indiscriminate attempt to "do everything".

On a day-to-day basis teachers need to keep selection in mind. The main criterion is *Will what I am going to say help these particular students?* Because *you* know it, it does not mean the students need to know it. There are two different problems — firstly the students may not need to know at *that time,* secondly they may not need to know *at all.* The textbook may, for example, present *on the left/right;* the teacher knows it is also possible to say *on* **your** *left/right.* To introduce this in a first presentation of "finding the way" would almost certainly confuse.

A more serious problem is that much of what language teachers have themselves learned is not relevant in the state school classroom. There are, as mentioned above, about 200 verbs in English with irregular past tense forms. Probably about 100 of these are in common use. It is helpful for students to learn these words in groups which are phonetically similar: *bring — brought — brought, catch — caught — caught.* Unfortunately it is then tempting for the teacher to present *complete* groups but while the student may need to know *speak — spoke — spoken,* there is less need for *weave — wove — woven.* The majority of school students, who will not go to university to study English, will *never* need about half of the verbs with irregular past forms *(cleave — clove — cloven).* Here is a clear case where teachers must select.

All teachers need to be careful of presenting too many alternative ways of saying something, of putting too much vocabulary on the board at the same time, of going too quickly and, finally, of telling students or giving them information which is not relevant to them. Stories of the teacher's recent visit to London may have a motivating effect on the class. They can also be very dull and boring.

The principle, as with each of the sections of this chapter, is that good teaching is not about showing students what you know, but about helping them to improve *their* knowledge, skills and performance.

10. Activities and relationships in the classroom change

Techniques for teaching specific language skills and handling particular lesson activities will be dealt with later in the book. Before looking at these particular techniques, however, it is worth stating a single general principle of language teaching — a "basic method". This can be done providing the reader bears in mind that it does not mean that all language teaching should always follow this method. It provides a general framework which systematises the common-sense approach.

If language learning is to be a natural and relatively relaxed process the general sequence will almost inevitably be:

Students meet new language in informal (natural) presentation.
Teacher presents the language formally.
Students use the language in formal, controlled practice.
Students use the language informally.

This approach can be expanded slightly into "a basic method".

1. The teacher uses structures or phrases which are intelligible in context before they are formally presented. This means that when the language is presented for active use by the student it is not completely unfamiliar. Students frequently acquire passively language which is later to be acquired actively.

2. The teacher draws specific attention to a particular language feature in a formal presentation. This process often involves the teacher giving an example, commenting upon it, asking and answering a question, etc. It may be summarised as the teacher "talking to himself" while the students eavesdrop. It is the teacher-to-teacher (T-T) phase.

3. The teacher questions the class as a whole and invites either a choral response, or a response from a volunteer within the group to indicate understanding, etc. This is the teacher-to-class (T-C) phase.

4. The teacher questions chosen individuals. This is teacher-to-student (T-S) phase. On occasion the roles are reversed and students question the teacher (S-T).

5. The students work with each other asking and replying to each other in more or less controlled pair work. In general the lesson develops from strictly controlled pair work, where each individual question and answer is predictable, to less controlled pair work where individual students have a wider range. This is the student-to-student (S-S) phase.

6. Frequently, the lesson then develops to a phase where students do individual (written) reinforcement, or to group activity. In both cases this phase is characterised by the fact that the teacher is not directly dominating the activity. The emphasis is either on work in small groups, or on the whole group working without direct teacher involvement. It is the group work phase.

In general two principles dominate this basic method — there is a development from controlled to free production, and there is a development from teacher-dominated to student-dominated activity.

The method may be summarised briefly as follows:

1. Informal use — T.
2. The teacher sets a pattern and replies — T-T.
3. The teacher questions the class and invites *them* to respond — T-C.
4. The teacher questions individual students — T-S.
5. Students work in pairs — S-S.
6. Group work.

Any activity involving 30 people could never be as simple or as linear in its development as the above method suggests. The method does, however, provide a fundamental pattern which will frequently be broken as individual decisions are made but which none-the-less represents an appropriate model for the general development of any class.

The classroom, and the language classroom in particular, should be a dynamic place — the lessons should be a lively, varied and involving experience. If it is to be dynamic in this sense, it is essential that teachers are aware that their relationship with the class is constantly changing. If the teacher always assumes a central, dominant role many of the activities essential to good language teaching will be automatically excluded.

11. Students need to learn how to learn

Many students studying a foreign language have very strange ideas of what will help them to improve. Most teachers have met students who think that by filling vocabulary books they will be able to speak better English; many students presented with a text will actually want to go through word-by-word and will not see the point of, for example, reading for gist, or scanning for particular information.

One of the tasks of the language teacher is to help the student to study more efficiently and more enjoyably. A small but important part of the teaching time should be spent making students aware of why certain things will help them, and why others will not. The more students understand about the process of learning the foreign language, the more they will be able to take responsibility for their own learning.

12. Useful *and* fun is better than either alone

Some language learning is not particularly enjoyable. Not many students enjoy committing a list of vocabulary to memory or doing long fill-in exercises, but learning a language is about *learning*, and cannot always be exciting and fun.

The other side of the story is equally true. Students are unlikely to be very successful at learning anything unless they enjoy the process. It is very clear that you cannot speak a foreign language well just by learning long lists of words, repeating mechanically after a tape recorder and so on.

Frequently, however, the distinction between useful exercises and "fun" is not as dramatic as teachers think. Good teachers try to ensure that as many activities as possible are both. Instead of a vocabulary test, why not play a vocabulary game; if students need to do written grammar practices, why not make some of the examples amusing.

Below is a logical puzzle. Many students will enjoy solving such puzzles in their own language and there is no reason why they shouldn't enjoy them in English. The activity, however, also has a very serious purpose. This particular puzzle can only be done if students make sentences such as *Peter went to Rome,* or *Peter didn't go to Rome.* It provides practice of negative forms. It has a serious, and carefully defined, structural purpose — but is still a puzzle, and still fun.

If the task itself is worth doing, and the students are actively involved, the activity is likely to fulfil a criterion which teachers should constantly keep in mind — it contains two questions compressed into one — *Is this usefun?*

Mike, David, Susan, Jane and Richard all went to different places for their holidays. They all travelled in different ways.

Who went to each place? How did each travel?

1. The person who went to Copenhagen went by plane. It was not David.
2. Susan went by boat.
3. The person who went to London cycled.
4. Jane went to Rome.
5. Mike went by car. He didn't go to Athens.

Fill in this table to help you.
Mark a ✔ if you know something *is* true.
Mark a X if you know something is *not* true.

	Rome	London	Paris	Copenhagen	Athens	Bike	Car	Train	Boat	Plane
David							X			
Mike					X		✔			
Susan							X			
Jane							X			
Richard							X			

13. We all learn best when we are relaxed

There is a big difference between learning your own language in the most natural way possible — in your pram or cot making no apparent effort, and the effort and concentration usually demanded in schools. Whatever teachers may think, it remains the case that we all learn best when we are mentally relaxed — open to the learning experience. If you feel pressurised, or tense, even if you perform at that moment, you will probably forget. Learning is a medium-to -long-term process, and we really retain language which we understand and feel involved with while we are 'open'. This is not to deny the value of concentration — but it does mean that teachers should always try to generate a relaxed atmosphere, inviting rather than demanding, a response.

14. Students can be silent, but still involved

Young (and not so young!) teachers tend to talk too much. In an effort to counteract this, training courses encourage them to reduce teacher talking time and increase student talking time. This is often justified on the grounds that 'it's the students who need the practice'. This advice is true — as far as it goes. Of course students should not be left listening to the teacher droning on, and of course students should be involved in the lesson. But that is very different from saying that all students should be encouraged to speak, or that the student who is not talking is not participating.

If you went to study any subject except a language, you would assume that you would spend most of your time listening — with no suggestion that this would be boring, or that you would not be involved. Students need plenty of opportunities to speak in language lessons, but teachers must avoid pressurising students into speaking — particularly if the students are adults. Some people naturally volunteer their views and ideas freely; others are more reflective personalities. It is the teacher's job to **involve** everybody, but not necessarily to involve everybody in the same way. Some students can participate fully while saying very little. This can be frustrating for the teacher, but it is important to realise that you are there to adapt to and help the students — not to impose your demands on them — creating stress and reducing learning— and certainly not in an effort to change their personalities.

If you are sensitive to the people around you, it is easy to tell the difference between students who are bored, and students who are silent but involved. In the former case, perhaps you need to change what you are doing; in the latter case, we suggest that you should respect the student's personal decision. Many students may genuinely enjoy listening to you, or to other students and, if they are relaxed, the language that they are hearing can be of real benefit to them. Learn to respect the fact that students may be involved in learning, without necessarily making a contribution to your idea of 'a good lesson'.

Chapter 2

Basic Principles 2 — Language and Language Learning

Mark each of these statements before and after you read the chapter.
Mark each statement
        ✔ if you *agree.*
        X if you *disagree.*
        ? if you are *undecided.*

1. *How* you say something is sometimes as important as *what* you say.	
2. It helps to contrast the students' native language with the target language.	
3. The difficulty of a text depends mostly on the vocabulary it contains.	
4. Natural conversation is too difficult for elementary students.	
5. Usually students should hear something before they say it or see it.	
6. It is never possible to say *This class has done the present perfect.*	
7. Students should not use their mother tongue in the lessons.	
8. Repetition is an important part of language learning.	
9. Teachers should use only English in the classroom.	
10. Structural mistakes should always be corrected.	

Basic Principles 2
Language and Language Learning

1. Language teaching is teaching language

A language is many things — it is a system, a code, a set of conventions, a means of communication, to mention only a few. Teachers of any subject must have a clear idea of the subject they are teaching — not only the facts of the subject, but also an overall view of the nature of the subject. This is as true for the language teacher as for any other teacher.

We have already expressed the view that learning is more important than teaching. Teaching should reflect the students' needs. It should also reflect the nature of the subject. Language is a complex phenomenon; it can be viewed as many different things. Good language teaching will reflect a variety of aspects of language.

Language is a system
Certain items in a language acquire meaning only by relation to other items in the language — words such as *I, with, which.* More importantly certain structures in the language can only be understood in contrast with other structures — in English, for example, the present simple and present continuous, or the past simple and present perfect. These aspects of language as a system need to be *understood and internalised.* They cannot simply be learned by heart if learners are ever going to be able to use the target language in an original way.

The teacher who understands language as a system will see the necessity for activities which lead to understanding.

Language is a habit
Many pieces of language are learned in quite large wholes (**A** *Hello, how are you?* **B** *Fine thanks. And you?* It is *normal* in many varieties of English for B to make a *positive* response, and follow with an enquiry about the other person.) Here the emphasis is not on understanding, but on the ability to respond automatically. The teacher who sees language as habit will see the necessity for repetition and intensive oral practice.

Language is a set of conventions
The positive response referred to above (*Fine thanks. And you?*) is part of a social convention. Social conventions vary from country to country. Using the social conventions of one coutnry in another may lead to embarrassment, confusion or misunderstanding. Such conventions are not only in the spoken language — a normal letter in English, even a business letter, begins *Dear . . . .*

The teacher who sees language as a set of conventions will see the necessity of contrasting the conventions of the language the student is learning with those of the student's own language or society.

Language is a means of communication

Most modern textbooks are based on "the communicative approach". The emphasis is on the fact that language is not used in a vacuum but by one person to another in order to communicate a message. This view seems obvious but the activities of the traditional language classroom ignored this aspect of language. Students frequently read texts in order to answer questions about the text. The *only* purpose of such texts was for the students to examine the language of text — the language of the textbook was not used to communicate anything else; the "comprehension" questions which followed such texts involved the students telling the teacher what the teacher already knew. If such activities were communicative in any way, they communicated not the content of the text, but the fact that the student had, or had not, mastered the language of the text. Nowadays it is generally agreed that concentrating on the language as a system "to be learned" is unnecessarily narrow. It is possible for students to study material of real interest to them, and to communicate real ideas of their own through the medium of the language they are learning.

Teachers who recognise language as communication will see the necessity for genuinely interesting texts, individualised teaching, pair work, free practices, listening practices and many other classroom activities.

A word of warning is, however, necessary. Communicative language teaching has sometimes been misunderstood and teachers have thought that, for example, *any* pair work is communicative. This is not the case. It is not the activity, but the *task* and the *purpose* for which the language is used, which make the activity authentically communicative.

Language is a means to an end

This is an extension of the idea of language as communication. Language is not used for its own sake; it is used for a purpose — to convey information, emotion or attitude; to help the memory in note taking; to entertain and instruct in a play; to explore feelings and understanding in poetry. The list of uses is almost endless but the important point for the language teacher is that language is used for a purpose.

At this point the nature of language connects to some of the important ideas in the previous chapter. If the teacher can identify the purpose for which the students need language, the teaching can be directed towards helping achieve those objectives. This seems obvious, but has very radical implications for much language teaching. Many students on a traditional course found that they knew a lot of structures but that they could not, for example, express irritation or other emotions in the language they had learned. Most elementary students of a foreign language will be reasonably good at conveying information but almost completely hopeless at conveying any sort of emotion. Perhaps some small syllabus changes could help students in this area.

The teacher who recognises language as a means to an end will see the necessity for looking at *why* particular pieces of language are useful and, having seen their purpose, will then be able to see their usefulness (or otherwise) for students. A simple example makes this much clearer — nursery rhymes are popular with young children, but *why* — what is their purpose? Their popularity rests on regular rhythms and rhymes. In other words, they are often excellent examples of the sound and stress system of the language. The teacher who sees this will soon see a use for them in the classroom; the teacher who simply thinks of them as "childish" will not see that use.

Language is a natural activity

People who study language sometimes talk about *language-like behaviour.* The term refers to the language often found in older textbooks or heard in too many classrooms:

A Is Peter shorter or taller than Alan?
B Alan is shorter than Peter.
A Ah, so Alan is not as tall as Peter.

The words are English; the structures are English but, somehow, we do not believe that two real people would *ever* talk to each other like that. In the same way textbooks contain texts which contain twelve uses of the present continuous and no other tense form. They are not language, they are language-like behaviour.

Teachers who recognise the distinction immediately see the absurdity of *Yes, that's right. Now can you say it in a whole sentence please?* This can be translated as *You have answered correctly using language,now please do it again using language-like behaviour*!

Language is a complex phenomenon; language teaching should reflect the different aspects of language. This should be quite enough to keep most students and teachers busy with their language lessons. Unfortunately, there are some things which language is *not*, and these should *not* interfere with language lessons.

English is not England.

For students who visit Britain, it can be interesting to know something about the country but it is equally important to remember that many students read English who will never visit Britain. For *some* students it may make sense to do an exercise which uses a map of London; for other students it may make more sense to use a map of their own home city. There is a temptation for many teachers — either native British teachers or teachers who have visited Britain, to think that what they know about Britain should form part of their English lessons. While all lessons are improved by the personal touch,teachers should remember they are primarily teaching language, not culture.

English is not a syllabus

School systems either have an explicit syllabus, often structurally arranged, or a syllabus which is defined by an examination system. There are exams, which are important for students, and teachers clearly need to take account of the exam requirements. This does not, however, mean that 'English' can be identified with the examination syllabus. As far as possible it should be the students' needs, and the real nature of language, which influence what happens in the classroom, not the arbitrary definitions of an examination system which, unfortunately rather too frequently, is out of date or inappropriate.

English is not "my" English

Native speakers have a tendency to believe that "because I say it", a language item could, or even should, be taught to students. Language teaching is about *selection*, and the criterion *I say it* is a very poor one.

Non-native teachers have a similar problem — they have a tendency to believe that because they know something, their students also need to know it. This may mean introducing 'exceptions' to students too early, giving alternative ways of saying things, giving correct but confusing information (*Subway in British English means a way under the road, but it's the word for an underground train in American English. In British English that's called a tube. All of that is true, but do students need to know it?*)

Perhaps most teachers should remind themselves once a week that whatever English is, it is not an opportunity for them to show off what they know in the classroom.

English is not an aesthetic experience

Many non-native language teachers have studied English extensively and have achieved a very high standard themselves. They may have taken real pleasure in studying Shakespeare, Dickens, or modern poetry. For the majority of their students, however, such an idea of English is very far away. Students may be studying English in order to read economics or chemistry; they may be studying it for practical reasons to do with improving their job prospects, or they may be studying it simply becuase they have to. Such students are hardly likely to be encouraged if teachers try to promote the view that, for example, "English is a beautiful language". This is simply another way of the teacher showing off.

As far as possible everything which happens in the classroom should be influenced by two decisive criteria:

Is this going to help these students to achieve their objectives?
Does this activity reflect the nature of language?

Language is a means to an end; language teaching is, therefore, a means to a means to an end. It is all too easy for teachers to lose sight of the ultimate goals of their activity. They will remain close to these if they constantly think of their students, and the nature of language.

2. Languages are different

Languages are different in the obvious sense that a certain object is referred to as *a table* in English, *ett bord* in Swedish, and *ein tisch* in German, but also often more fundamentally in the way they systematise reality.

The difference may occur in any feature of the language. Many European languages possess two (or more) words which are the equivalent of the single English word *you*. English possesses two possibilities for "the present tense":
I *think* so.   *I'm thinking* about it.
while most European languages possess only one form equivalent in part to both of the English forms.

Once outside the group of closely-associated European languages, differences appear in many other areas. Here are some more unusual examples:

In Chinese intonation can change the actual meaning of a word — MA said on a level pitch means *mother*, but with a rise of pitch means *horse*.

Certain languages employ grammatical categorisations which mean that the 'obvious' distinction between a noun and a verb in English is not used.

Finnish does not use prepositions, but its nouns have an enormous number of different forms (cases).

Russian does not possess articles.

Pronouns are frequently omitted in spoken Italian where they would be necessary in English.

French adjectives agree with nouns while English adjectives do not change their form.

The list is almost endless.

While language teachers do not need to be concerned with possible variations, they do need to recognise that they cannot take for granted that students will be able to see differences which are 'obvious' to native speakers, or those with a good knowledge of English.

In general, students tend to assume that the language they are learning behaves similarly to their own native language. This assumption will result in them making interference mistakes — carrying over the patterns of their own language inappropriately to the language they are learning. Teachers need, over a period of time and in different ways, to persuade students that languages *are* different and that they must not be surprised by differences.

When obvious differences occur, attention should be drawn to them in the teaching. More generally, however, students should be discouraged from word-for-word translation and encouraged to understand, and to *feel* that learning a foreign language is learning to see the world through new eyes.

3. Language is what, how and why

Although most course books are arranged structurally, knowing a language is much more than knowing the structures. The language can be seen in many ways, but for teaching purposes three are particularly important — vocabulary and structures are *what* is said; pronunciation, stress and intonation are *how* it is said, and function is *why* it is said. Good teaching needs to take account of all three.

The words 'structure' and 'grammar' are often mixed up but there is an important difference in their meaning. In the spoken language stress and intonation are part of the grammar of the language and often contribute as much as structure to meaning :

A Is there anything else we need?   **A** Milk and sugar?
B Milk and sugar.   **B** Please.

Structures are frequently not equivalent from language to language. The same is also true of stress and intonation patterns and of how language functions are realised in different languages.

English, for example, frequently indicates doubt by a rising intonation at the end of a verb phrase; this is not true in many other languages.

Similarly, English possesses a word which marks the difference between a normal and an abrupt request — *please*—while a language as close to English as Swedish does not possess this; conversely many European languages possess a phrase directly associated with the act of offering — *s'il vous plâit, bitte* — while English does not.

A course which concentrates too much on structure will leave students with an unbalanced knowledge of English. Language teachers need to maintain a balance so students are aware of, and practise, each of structure, stress and intonation, and function. Although individual practices frequently concentrate on one or other of these, the teacher should constantly have all three in mind and be prepared to add comments to preserve a balance.

4. 'Level' is a complex idea

Students learning a foreign language follow a syllabus; this may be defined by a ministry of education, by the school, or by the textbook being followed. With the exception of students who are learning a language while visiting the country where it is spoken, however, most students will be exposed to the language in some sort of step-by-step approach. If the syllabus is designed with reference only to structure this approach creates no problem. The syllabus lists and sequences the structures the student needs to "know". It is possible to say that students 'have done the present perfect' and that the next step is the present perfect continuous. Unfortunately, we have already seen that language is much more than structure, so any syllabus based *only* on structure will have serious defects.

As soon as the *use* of language is introduced, the concept of level becomes much more difficult. Here are some of the factors which make language 'difficult':
1. The occurrence of a lot of words the reader or listener does not know.
2. Reading a text which is written in complex rather than simple sentences.
3. Reading a text written in a particular style — newspaper headlines, official letters, scientific reports.
4. Listening to a non-standard or unfamiliar accent.
5. The *density* of new language or new ideas.
6. The length of the text, either written or spoken.
In addition to all of these factors, there is, from the language teaching point of view, the difficulty of the *task* which the student is asked to perform. There is, for example, a difference between having to understand every word of a text, being able to give a general idea of its meaning, and being able to provide an accurate precis of it; there is a difference between having to understand *all* the details of a recorded talk or dialogue and being able to answer a single specific question.

Traditional elementary language teaching material was always written specially. Language presented to students in the early stages of learning was specially 'processed' using structural criteria. As the level of course increased, more complicated structures were introduced and texts grew longer but, on the whole, the tasks the students were asked to perform remained similar.

Modern methods suggest a wider concept of level is better. A clear distinction, for example, needs to be made between what students must *produce* and what they must understand. As soon as this is accepted, material which is structurally beyond the students' productive level may be introduced to practise *understanding*. This means the whole process of language learning can be made more natural — real materials, using natural language, can be introduced into a course at a much lower level than would be possible if only structural criteria were considered. Students can be set real, yet simple, tasks based on authentic material. Sometimes teachers with a strongly structural background themselves are confused by this modern approach. It means, for example, that instructions given to students in their textbook may include structures which the students have not officially met as part of their 'learning for production' syllabus.

The principle is that level is a combination of factors — the length, density and content of the material and, perhaps most importantly, the difficulty of the task which the student has to perform.

5. Natural language has a place in all courses

Once the wider concept of level just discussed has been accepted, it is self-evident that there is opportunity to provide a more natural and interesting basis for language learning at all levels by introducing authentic material. Teachers who themselves learned a language through a traditional structure-based course will recall the frustration of reaching a good intermediate level in their classroom studies, only to be disappointed when faced for the first time with trying to use their language in a natural situation — perhaps either on a visit to a country where the language was spoken, with a native speaker, or when their teacher finally 'dared' to bring an authentic text or tape into the classroom.

Of course it is necessary to pre-select and arrange the materials for text-books. There are strong arguments for using materials which have been specially written, but not exclusively so. If students are ever to use the language outside the classroom, such pre-selection is not possible. A student may ask a simple question but there is no way of making sure that the reply is also simple. The beginners' textbook may have taught answers to *Excuse me, can you tell me the way to ... please?* but the student who asks for Crowther Road in a real situation may meet the answer *Are you going to the match then?* The student visiting Britain has to understand the same timetable or menu as the one used by native speakers. Even if the textbook has not explained the meaning of *sats ex* students will need to understand it if they are to avoid being late for the performance!

Real materials show students that, even at the earliest stages of their learning, what they are learning is useful outside the classroom. They also reassure students that what they are studying is real. Too often, particularly in state schools, a foreign language is not something real; it is a subject on the timetable three times a week, a strange intellectual game played with one of the teachers.

For all these reasons, it is a good idea to introduce something real into the classroom — a *short* tape-recording of natural speech, or a piece of real printed material — a timetable, an advert, menu, form, etc. — even if such material may *in one sense* be 'too difficult' for the student.

The principle is that providing the task the students are asked to perform with this material is sufficiently simple, such materials are motivating, and ensure that the subject seems more lively and real for students at *all* levels.

6. Knowing the language is not enough

Every classroom activity should have a specific linguistic purpose. All natural language use has a purpose — to give information, to express emotion, to advance an argument, etc. A moment's thought reveals that much of the language of the language classroom does not have a purpose in this way. Isolated sentences practise forms and are intended to encourage the student to remember the form, but they have no real communicative purpose. As far as possible, classroom activities should be planned so that they do have a real, natural communicative purpose.

The purpose of many language teaching texts is to present language. This use never occurs outside the language classroom. It is better to present the language in a text which is studied for a purpose other than language itself. The student who is interested in learning to windsurf will be more motivated to work with a text which teaches him how to windsurf than a text which presents examples of the present perfect. Nobody reads a recipe without wondering if they will enjoy the dish!

The most effective language teaching will mean that the students are set realistic tasks where they *use* language for a purpose rather than manipulate it for its own sake.

An approach which is based on the performance of tasks both more accurately reflects the nature of language, and is more likely to boost the students' self-confidence. Many students who "fail" or are de-motivated by an approach based on language for its own sake, increase in confidence, and are highly motivated by, an approach which is based on realistic tasks. The importance of the boost to students' confidence cannot be over-estimated.

7. Most language skills can be divided into sub-skills

We have seen that level depends on more than the structures used. Among other things it also depends on the length of the text and the difficulty of the task. One of the skills of language *teaching,* is to help students by breaking down large tasks into smaller, more detailed, tasks and selecting the correct length of 'text'. (The term 'text' refers here to either a printed text, or a recording).

Traditional language teaching has concentrated on the sentence. Modern theory and research have shown that this is not sufficient, for at least two reasons. Firstly, the student who understands individual sentences will not necessarily be able to transfer that knowledge to the understanding of extended (printed) text. Extended text has certain features which do not occur in individual sentences — for example, paragraphs beginning with a 'topic sentence' which is then expanded; the relation between general statements and examples in certain types of academic writing; the use of certain words and phrases to structure extended text (*on the other hand, however, in a similar way, conversely).*

The same problem applies to dialogue — certain language uses are characteristic of *responses* so that if teaching concentrates on individual sentences such important uses will never occur. A simple example is the manipulative use of the auxiliary in dialogues such as:

A I've just got back from holiday.   **A** We went to Brittany.
B Oh have you? Where did you go?   **B** Oh did you? Did you have a good
time?

The second difficulty is rather different; examination of transcripts of natural conversation show that people very rarely speak in full sentences. A single speaker often piles phrases or clauses one on top of the other; alternatively, speakers may 'interrupt' each other using part of what the previous speaker said to complete their own idea. At the same time natural conversation is not a disorganised jumble of phrases; on the contrary, it is carefully structured but, and here is the important point, the structure extends beyond the single sentence and even beyond the single 'turn' of one speaker.

In summary, natural text is structured at different levels — phrases, sentences, paragraphs, and even larger units such as a whole chapter of a book or a complete lecture. The ability to use a language, both receptively and productively, implies an understanding of the structure of such small units as phrases, and such large units as chapters. Traditional language teaching has tended to concentrate on only two units — the sentence (for structure), and the individual phoneme (for pronunciation). If language teaching is to reflect what language really is, and how it is used, teachers need to be aware of a wider range of structural devices, and a wider range of skills which students need in order to encode and decode language successfully. Here are some examples:

If a student's language does not possess the distinction between /p/ and /b/ and the teacher says *No, not bin, pin. Listen, not bin, pin* and the student promptly repeats *bin* it is easy to assume that the student cannot make the sound /p/; in fact, it is possible that the student cannot *hear* the distinction. The skill of recognition precedes that of production. If teachers are in any doubt about this they should consider the difficulty they would face (assuming they do not write Arabic) in copying an Arabic sentence accurately — the difficulty is we are not sure which of the "dots and squiggles" are significant; without recognising what is important, it is a matter of chance whether or not it is accurately reproduced. Too often teaching fails to make the distinction between recognition and production.

Another difficulty applies with listening. Listening is a global term; it involves everything that we hear — sounds, stress patterns, intonation, changes of pitch, etc. The whole message is conveyed by a combination of these factors. Frequently language teachers assume that students' understanding of what they hear is global; in fact it can be broken down into sub-skills. A single word repeated on a high pitch in English, for example, can be used to show surprise. A simple teaching sequence such as the following makes this clear for students:

Students listen to a tape of a two-line dialogue:

A We're going to Kenya for our holidays.
B Kenya!

The teacher asks:
Where are they going for their holiday? *(Kenya).*
How does B feel! *(Surprised).*
How do you know? *(His voice goes up a lot).*

This simple sequence ensures that the teacher breaks down the general skill of understanding (B is surprised) by drawing attention to the sub-skill (listen to pitch, and pitch change).

In the case of listening, the question pair *How does X feel? How do you know?* will often ensure the student can understand/interpret a response and, through the second question, be led to an awareness of the *source* of such understanding.

In a similar way students can be encouraged to see the details of the way a written text is structured by the teacher asking questions about the use of structuring words such as *conversely, moreover, despite.* In such cases it is appropriate for the teacher to ask students what sort of idea the writer is going to express next. Once again, the general problem of 'understanding the text' can be broken down into a sequence of more specific problems.

The principle is that almost all language skills, both receptive and productive, can be broken down into sub-skills through the use of specific questions. Teachers must recognise that it is unrealistic to ask students to go from writing a sentence to writing an essay, or from answering a question to engaging in natural conversation. Students need to be helped by being shown, and specifically taught, the structure of a paragraph, how to link what they have said to the previous speaker, etc. Skills need to be broken into sub-skills, and teaching needs to build from small units to larger, not leap from a detail to the whole.

8. Hear, speak, read, write is a good sequence

Of course there can be no absolute rules for the "best" order for presentation of the four skills. In general, however, in the case of English where spelling is often confusing, the sequence above is usually best. It is interesting to note that this sequence is not the one employed in most school systems, at least until recently. Many students started with written text, did written exercises which encouraged their own writing skills, and only subsequently listened to the natural language and spoke themselves.

Consideration of how people learn their own language soon leads to the obvious primacy of listening. Some modern theoreticians make the distinction between language learning (conscious) and language acquisition (unconscious). If this distinction is accepted, it is clear that listening once again assumes particular significance as, in addition to what is listened to, much of what is only heard influences the unconscious acquisitional process.

Some radical experiments have been done which suggest that it is possible to teach a language successfully while requiring very little of the productive skills from the students during the early stages of teaching. Carefully selected listening and reading passages, chosen so that the majority of the content will be comprehensible to the students, help acquisition and build the students' confidence in their ability to "manage" the foreign langauge. These effects are seen later when students make better than average progress in the productive skills.

Writing a word on the blackboard before students say it can create unnecessary problems. Try to follow the pattern *"say then see"*.

If you use the blackboard for pronunciation practices, use phonetics or quasi-phonetics.

A sound can often be represented by several different spellings. /ʃ/, for example, can appear as "sh", "ss" or "ti". The last seems to bear little resemblance to the actual sound and, if the word *station* is on the blackboard, merely pointing at the word will not necessarily help students to produce the right sound.

If students know the phonetic symbols, use these. If not, represent the sounds by using quasi-phonetics. The initial sound of *judge* may, for example, be represented by "dy" and students helped by asking them to repeat the sequence:

yes, d-yes, dy, dy

Without being dogmatic about a sequence it is helpful to bear the above, and in particular the primacy of listening, in mind.

9. Language learning is cyclical

Old-fashioned syllabuses assumed that language learning was linear; the structures of the language were presented in a single sequence. There came a point when students had 'done the present perfect'. Nowadays nobody believes language learning is linear; the same language item needs to be studied again and again throughout a course. There are at least three reasons why this needs to be done:

a. Learners forget, so straightforward revision is necessary from time to time.

b. Additional uses of a structure need to be studied — irregular past tense forms are needed to form the past simple, but are also needed in many conditional sentences.

c. Most importantly of all, but the reason which is most frequently overlooked, is that as learners advance they need to *deepen* their understanding. It may, for example, be a good idea to teach the present simple for repeated actions and the present continuous for actions at the moment of speaking at one stage of a student's course, but this is in no sense *the* reason for using these tense forms. Nor is this an explanation of the fundamental difference between the two verb forms. As students meet uses which contradict that explanation (for example, the present continuous referring to future time, *I'm playing tennis on Saturday;* the present simple to refer to momentary actions precisely at the moment of speaking, *Ah, now I see what you mean)* it is necessary to re-examine *all* previous study of, in this case, the present simple and present continuous, so that students gradually build up a comprehensive view of the underlying difference in the use of these forms. It is unreasonable to expect that they will do this by having **a** particular difference explained to them when they first meet the form, and then allowing students to meet examples of different uses. Language is a system and, if the teaching is to reflect this, teachers must be prepared to return again and again to examining certain fundamental problems of the language. Structural examples in English would be the difference between countable and uncountable nouns, the difference between continuous and non-continuous forms, and the difference between present perfect and past simple.

The cyclical nature of language learning is not, however, confined to structure; it relates to all areas of language learning. A simple and obvious example is pronunciation. There is no guarantee that, once students have produced a sound in the language correctly they will never mis-pronounce it again; on the contrary, certainty of pronunciation comes only after long practice.

We have already discussed that the concept of level is partly a question of *extent.* It is also, as students improve, a question of *appropriacy* — it may be sufficient for beginners to "say what they mean" using the few words and phrases at their disposal but, as their language progresses, the language chosen should be appropriate. In conversation, for example, this will mean they learn not simply to answer questions, but also to take more initiatives. An understanding of this is reflected in cyclical language teaching not from week to week, but with a short sequence within a single lesson. An example would be the use of communicative pairwork — pairs of students are asked to do an information gap problem. One of the pairs is asked to 'perform' their dialogue for the class. All of the class are then invited to comment — not only on "mistakes", but also on alternative, better ways of saying things and, most importantly of all, on anything which the pair missed out completely. Another pair is then asked to perform, avoiding the mistakes and producing a fuller, more natural, version of the dialogue. If necessary the process is repeated. A practice of this kind is not finished when it has been done once, it needs to be repeated both in the lesson, on a short term cycle, and, perhaps, a number of lessons later, on a longer-term cycle.

Teachers and students are well aware that doing exactly the same thing twice is boring. It is therefore of particular importance that teachers recognise that the "repeats" within any cyclical learning are *not* exact repeats — each repeat must be a development. Teachers must not be afraid of doing what seems to the students the same thing more than once. If it does appear so to the students then the teacher should be prepared to explain *why* something is being done again, and *how* the repeat will be different from the previous performance. The path from knowing nothing to being able to perform naturally and spontaneously is a difficult one. It is essential for students to go forward step-by-step and, if there are difficulties, to repeat those steps which they find difficult.

Very often students find the earliest stages of learning a foreign language fun because they feel they are making considerable progress. After a while progress seems slower and the excitement is lost. Teachers can help students at this level by emphasising that language learning is not only about learning new language, but also about learning to perform more difficult tasks with the language you already know.

Language learning does not consist of piling little bricks of knowledge one on top of the other. The process is more complicated than that and involves revising, extending knowledge of the use of, and extending understanding of things which you have already met.

10. Language is used for different purposes in the classroom

Consider a lesson which starts in the following way:

T is the teacher, **C** is the whole class, **S1, S2** etc. individual students.

T	Good morning everbody, please sit down.
C	Good morning.
T	Now, S1, did you watch the game last night?
S1	I didn't go, but I seed it on TV.
T	You did what?
S1	I seed it on TV
T	Seed? Is that right? . . . remember, it's irregular . . . We say watch, watched, but we don't say see, seed. What do we say . . . ?
S2	Saw.
T	That's right, saw. So what did you do S1?

S1   I saw it on TV.
T   Good. Everybody say that please.
C   I saw it on TV.
T   What about you, S3? Did you go or did you see it on TV?

It is easy to see that the teacher's language is used for very different reasons here. What begins socially — perhaps the class talked in a previous lesson about some local sport — soon becomes teaching where the teacher has to correct, give an example, give an instruction, comment and explain.

In a chemistry lesson nobody confuses what is being taught (chemistry) with the medium which is being used to teach it, but such confusion can arise in an English lesson. Teachers should try always to be aware of *why* they are using a particular piece of language in the lesson. If students are going to use the language item it must be suitable for their active vocabulary. On the other hand there is no reason at all why the teacher should not use language socially which is outside the students' present active knowledge (*What are you up to?* when a student is caught doing something unexpected).

Many British schoolteachers rely heavily on irony and pleasant sarcasm to create the general atmosphere of their classes and even as a feature of discipline. This kind of linguistic behaviour is very sophisticated — often depending on wide knowledge of the language, slang, and an ear for intonation. It is easy to see that it is therefore inappropriate to introduce this kind of linguistic behaviour into foreign language classes.

This does not mean that classes need to be humourless — visual jokes, jokes which depend upon the relationship between you and your students, and funny stories, where the joke has a narrative line, can all be used. Linguistic jokes, on the other hand, will usually fall flat, and not infrequently result in you being asked for explanations which turn out to be long, rambling, and slightly embarrassing!

The principle is that teachers need, even in the hurly-burly of a lesson, to be aware of the function of the different things they are saying if they are to avoid swamping their students with unnecessary and confusing language.

11. Do not be afraid of the students' mother tongue

There is a real danger in word-for-word translation but this does not mean that it is a good idea to ban the students' mother tongue from the classroom. There are situations where the students' mother tongue is of particular use:

a. If students need to discuss a difficulty with the teacher, and the teacher understands and can speak the students' mother tongue well, there is no reason to make the discussion artificially difficult by insisting that it takes place in English.

b. If students are working in groups preparing or discussing material and all the students have the same mother tongue it is *not* essential that the whole discussion takes place in English. While this may be desirable, with most classes it is sufficient to ensure the activity is useful if the reports of the groups, and the *general* class discussion of the individual group reports, is in English.

There are considerable advantages to allowing both languages in the classroom — some students will have ideas but not the English to express them; others will have the English but not the ideas. Permitting both languages — preferably in clearly defined areas — usually ensures that much of the work is more interesting, and that ultimately a higher standard of English is achieved.

12. Motor skills need practice

Language is a complicated phenomenon, and language learning a complicated process. It involves skills of different types, and some of these skills are purely physical. Recognising and making the distinction between /b/ and /p/, or /l/ and /r/, if you are not familiar with these distinctions in your own language, requires a lot of practice.

At all stages of learning, but particularly the early stages, students need a lot of practice of simply "getting their tongues around the words". Traditional question and answer techniques are very inefficient for this. Teachers can immediately improve by making it a *general* practice to ask the whole class to repeat new words in chorus, or to repeat the correct answer after an individual student has given it.

Asking for repetitions in this way need not slow the class up. If students understand that they are regularly expected to repeat a new item chorally two or three times, after it has been introduced, such practice can serve to bring the class together and to speed up lessons.

For those students whose writing system does not use the same alphabet as English there will be similar difficulties in the motor skills associated with writing.

Teachers who have been brought up on "a communicative approach" sometimes forget the importance of practising basic motor skills. If you cannot articulate what you want to say, or if your writing is completely illegible, you will communicate nothing!

13. Distinguish clearly between accuracy and fluency practices

Language learning has two distinct objectives — learning to use the language as an effective means of communication, and, more formally, using the language accurately. To some extent the two objectives overlap — the student who makes *too* many mistakes will not communicate well. On the other hand, it is frequently possible, and for some students necessary, to communicate effectively even if the message contains a fairly high proportion of formal errors.

Traditional language teaching placed a great emphasis on accuracy and teachers were encouraged to correct mistakes. The mistakes they corrected were almost always those which the students had positively made — mostly errors of pronunciation and structure. Mistakes which students did not make — omissions — things they did not even attempt to say — were not "corrected". Teachers worried a lot about *when* to correct — immediately a mistake was made, or as a follow-up after the end of a practice.

The dilemma has become more acute as more and more emphasis is placed on communicative language teaching. This has resulted, for example, in more students doing pair or group work. Most teaching sequences now involve both controlled and free practices.

Most of the dilemmas are solved providing the teacher has clearly in mind a single distinction — is the emphasis of this activity on *accuracy,* or on *fluency*?

There is a tendency for teachers to believe beginners require only accuracy practice, and more advanced students *only* fluency practice. This is not true — the best language teaching offers both kinds of practice at all levels.

Teachers should make clear to their students that in a practice which concentrates on accuracy *all* important mistakes will be corrected. Accuracy practices are essentially classroom activities — they place the emphasis on language *learning.* They are, unfortunately, not very exciting, but are an important part of the learning process.

In fluency practices teachers must *not* correct every mistake, and indeed must positively encourage students to use all means at their disposal to get their message across. If this involves using their hands, drawing, making up new words, etc. this is all to the good. This is what people do in real life when they have to get a message across in a language they know only imperfectly.

14. Interesting communicative tasks increase motivation

Speaking a foreign language is a complex skill. Not surprisingly language teachers try to simplify for their students. Sometimes, however, the process of simplification can be counter-productive. Very few interesting texts contain only one tense form and no natural conversation occurs in which the speakers concentrate entirely on structure and ignore intonation. In some ways, as soon as the language is dissected, like the rabbit which is dissected in the laboratory, it is dead. While the biology teacher can justify dissecting *one* rabbit, it is important to remember that most children would rather play with rabbits than dissect them.

Sometimes the language teacher can justify dissecting what is happening. It may help to isolate a structure, to practise irregular forms, to repeat difficult sounds, etc. Such activities, however, are a long way from ensuring that the students can understand and use the language. There is a danger that too much formal activity of this kind ensures that students can go through the "tricks" which are part of their examination, but which have little to do with developing their ability to use a foreign language naturally.

One of the principal ways the teacher moves in the direction of more highly motivating language teaching, and teaching which is more likely to affect the students' general ability to use the language, is to dissect less, and to pay more attention to setting students *tasks* which develop the skills necessary to find a solution.

The tasks may be of many different kinds. The following are only a few examples:

1. If tourists or other visitors are to be found in your town students can prepare a questionnaire then go out and interview people.

2. Students can prepare a simple guide to their town or region. Why should they do this in English? — ideally you should agree to stencil it then, for example, distribute it through the information centre or some of the larger hotels.

3. If students are studying a particular area in another subject, you can integrate the topic you are studying with what they are doing in, for example, history or physics. They can use English language material from the library to gather information relevant to their other subjects.

4. Small groups within the class can be given a piece of authentic material — from, for example, a British Travel Association brochure. Students then pre-pare a list of questions about the text. Groups exchange texts and try to pare a list of questions about the text. Groups exchange texts and try to answer the questions set by the other group. The competitive element in this task is itself a motivation.

5. Individual students can be asked to complete a simple questionnaire, such as that given below, then students exchange questionnaires and report the results of each other's to the whole class.

My birthday is on _____

My favourite month of the year is _____

The nicest time of the year for a holiday is _____
_____

because _____

The three most important dates every year for me are: _____ , _____ , **and**_____ **because** __
_____

---

6. Most younger students are curious about the world around them. A list such as the following which they have simply to mark T (true) or F (false) will interest them. At the same time this particular list provides good presenta-tion material for the present simple.

Are these True or False? Mark each one ✔ if you think it is true or X if you think it is false.

1. Horses and hippopotamuses belong to the same family.
2. African elephants sleep standing up, so they stand up for over 50 years.
3. Bats see with their ears, not their eyes.
4. The tallest living animal is the giraffe.
5. When mice have babies, they usually have more than twelve at a time.
6. Rabbits sometimes have up to a hundred young in a year.

7. Almost all problem solving activities (three examples are given below) are more interesting and motivating than text used only for language presentation.

> Can you answer these questions. The obvious answer is always wrong!
>
> **a.** A clock strikes six in five seconds. How long does it take to strike twelve? (*Not* 10 seconds).
>
> **b.** A fast train leaves London for Brighton at the same time as a slow train leaves Brighton for London. The fast train goes at 70mph. The slow train goes at 40mph. It is 50 miles from London to Brighton. Which train is further from London when they meet?
>   You can do this in your head — no pen or paper!
>
> **c.** There are 100 sweets in a small box. The sides of a big box are twice as long as the sides of a short box. How many sweets does a big box hold? (*not* 200).

Some of the tasks mentioned may be performed in English, while others may be performed in a mixture of English and the student's native language, or even entirely in the student's native language. It is *not* essential that such activities are performed exclusively in English — that is not the purpose of such activity. The tasks themselves are motivating and can only be done if students understand, *and can use,* what they have read or heard in English. The performance of the task is itself a worthwhile activity and ensures that students have used their English. If they write or report in English this is a bonus.

15. You learn to speak by listening

Think of your first language — you learned it, without any effort, with nobody asking you to repeat or formally correcting you. In the most obvious way possible, you mastered a very difficult skill — you learned to speak your own language simply by listening to it. Second language learning is not as different as people sometimes pretend; again, the best way to learn is through good listening.

Of course you can't just listen to anything — it's not like having water sprayed over you which you simply absorb. You need to understand some, and preferably most of what you hear; you need to be interested, and therefore involved. In the jargon, you need to be exposed to good 'input', but unless you are involved, and relaxed that input will not become 'intake'. We have already remarked in the previous chapter that you can be fully involved without necessarily talking very much — it is very important to realise that if your students are listening well, and are involved in what they are listening to, you are benefiting them not only in developing their listening skills, but also their general language level.

Chapter 3

Classroom Management and General Tips

Mark each of these statements before and after you read the chapter.
Mark each statement
> ✔ if you *agree*.
> X if you *disagree*.
> ? if you are *undecided*.

1. The best place for the teacher is standing at the front of the classroom.	
2. "I like busy lessons — with as little silence as possible."	
3. Pair work is only useful if everybody is using the target language.	
4. "I don't mind if they speak their own language in group work."	
5. In new work always ask students "Do you understand?"	
6. I talk too much in my lessons.	
7. If I don't know the answer, I tell the students I don't know.	
8. Never go systematically 'round the class' with practices.	
9. The overhead projector is particularly useful for showing *pictures*.	
10. Tapes and videos always make the lesson more interesting.	

Classroom Management and General Tips

1. Arrange the seating to help

The spoken language is about people talking to each other. If students are sitting in straight lines facing the back of each other's necks this is not easy to do!

Fortunately it isn't a rule that students have to sit like that. You should be prepared to re-arrange the desks — both for your language lessons and sometimes even for a particular activity — so that it is both easier and more natural for students to see and talk to each other.

For the typical adult class of perhaps between 5 and 15 students one of the following arrangements would probably be best.

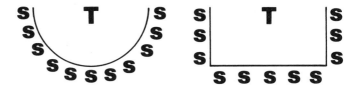

For a school class of perhaps 30 it is probably best to use the conventional arrangement for activities which are centered upon the teacher, but to allow students to move either their desks or at least their chairs for pair and group work.

If pair and group work is a novelty, students will take a long time to move and find the moving itself more interesting than the group work which follows. If, on the other hand, pair and group work is a normal part of your teaching, students will move naturally, quickly and quietly to new positions providing they know what they have to do and understand that this is not an opportunity to waste time but a useful and enjoyable activity.

The seating should suggest that students are encouraged to talk to each other; at the same time, it should allow for the removal of the teacher from a central, dominant role during certain activities.

2. Stand up when you're directing activity

In general it is only a good idea to sit down in a language class on two occasions; firstly if the students are doing something which, for the moment, does not involve you. The second occasion is if you are having a conversation or discussion with the class. If you remain standing, it is all too easy for you to

dominate and inhibit the students. On such occasions, once you have introduced and started the activity, it is usually better to sit either at, or on, your
desk.

For most activities in the language classroom it is important that the
students can see you and, in particular, your mouth and eyes. This is much
easier if you are standing. Standing also means you can see all the students
clearly and can use your eyes and hands effectively.

3. Look at the students

There is no more certain way to lose the attention of your students than to
take your eyes off them for long periods. This is not because they will get up
to mischief if you are not looking, but because normal human contact
frequently depends on, and is reinforced by, eye contact.

If you are standing, and your eyes are constantly moving over the class,
everyone feels involved. Your eyes help your students' concentration!

Your eyes can be used instead of your hands to indicate who should
answer a question, whether something is right or wrong, to encourage, etc. If
you can use your eyes effectively, you will find it easier to avoid using unnecessary language.

It is particularly important to remember that the easiest way to check
whether your students understand what you have said, or what they have
read or heard, is for your eyes to look at theirs. Any incomprehension or
confusion will show in their eyes long before they *tell* you that there is a
problem.

4. Use your hands to encourage and direct students

There are three main ways of showing students what you want — your voice,
your eyes, and your hands. There are two main reasons for using your hands
— you avoid unnecessary language which can distract students and, while
remaining completely clear, your hands can be used to increase the pace of
the lesson.

A simple gesture can indicate who is going to answer a question, or which
pair of students should now read a dialogue. Simple gestures can also indicate that something is wrong — for example, holding up one hand and shaking
it from side to side — or that a student should repeat something — a circular
"rolling" motion with one hand.

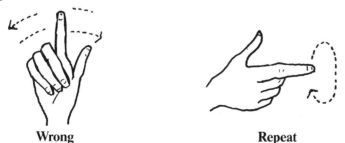

Wrong   **Repeat**

Such gestures, used but not over-used, provide a reassuring structure for
students and mean that you can indicate what is required from individual
students, or even from the whole class, with a minimum of fuss.

In directing the whole class the movement should be bold enough and decisive enough for all to see; in directing an individual student the gestures must be on a much smaller scale so that they appear invitations rather than authoritarian directives.

5. Use the back of your hand to point

If you point in the conventional way it can appear aggressive and inhibit students. Using the back of your hand to gesture is less intimidating, and conveys an invitation rather than a directive.

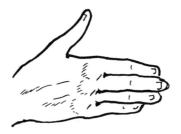

6. Use pauses to punctuate what you say

Try to read the following:

> Listen to this example was she there yes she was listen again was she there yes she was but now listen to this does she know him yes she does notice in the first was she yes she was and in the second example does she yes she does if there's was in the question there's was in the answer if there's does in the question there's does in the answer listen again.

It is very difficult to read anything if it is written like that. Writing is usually punctuated and the punctuation makes it easier to read. The example shows clearly that the teacher is using language for different purposes:

Listen again.	(Giving instructions)
Does she know him?	(Giving example)
Notice, in the first	(Commenting)

If the teacher speaks "without punctuation" in situations like this, students will be very confused. One of the main ways to provide this "spoken punctuation" is to make very short pauses before each change in the use of language from, for example, instruction to example. These pauses are an important feature of the way the teacher uses language in the classroom.

7. Vary your voice

This does not mean speaking in a 'funny voice'. It is important to mark the changes in why you are speaking. Pauses, stress and changes of pitch when you change from, for example, comment to instruction, will mean it is much easier to follow what you say. Even students whose level of English is not high can be taught in English providing the teacher does not use unnecessary language and providing the stream of speech is broken up by pauses and changes of voice.

The example given above should be *said* in such a way that it sounds more as this example appears when spaced on the page like this:

Listen to this example:
    Was she there?
    Yes she was.
Listen again:
    Was she there?
    Yes she was.
But now listen to this:
    Does she know him?
    Yes she does.
Notice, in the *first,* **was** she, Yes she **was**
And in the second example **does** she, yes she **does**
(Longer pause)
    If there's (pause) **was** in the question, there's **was** in the answer.
    If there's (pause) **does** in the question, there's **does** in the answer.

8. Keep your language to a minimum when students are doing something

If you speak, students will usually listen. If you want to encourage your students to use language, it obviously means that once you have introduced an activity and made clear what is wanted, you must be prepared to keep quiet. There are several important implications:

Do not interrupt students unnecessarily while they are preparing something.
Do not dominate discussions yourself.
Do not tell students what they want to say.
Do not use more language than is necessary to direct and control classroom activity.

We have already noted that you can reduce the amount of unnecessary classroom language by using your eyes and your hands. Sometimes verbal comment is called for, but even then there are good and bad ways of doing it. Oral exercises are a particular problem. Compare these two versions:

Version 1
T   So we don't just say 'no', we say 'I'm afraid not'. Can you all say that together please. Are you ready? Altogether please. Everybody, I'm afraid not.
C   I'm afraid not.
T   Yes that was very good. Now, can you say it, please S1.
S1 I'm afraid not.
T   Yes, very good. That was good, yes. Now you please, can you say it please S2?

Version 2

T	So not, 'no', but 'I'm afraid not'. Listen — I'm afraid not. Say it together please.
C	I'm afraid not.
T	Again.
C	I'm afraid not.
T	*(gestures to S1)*
S1	I'm afraid not.
T	*(nods, gestures to S2)*
S2	I'm afraid not.
T	*(gestures No, and Again)*
S2	I'm afraid not.
T	*(smiles, nods, gestures to S3)*
S3	I'm afraid not.
T	Good, everybody.
C	I'm afraid not.

The secret is simple — the verbal instructions are given using the imperative. This automatically avoids unnecessary language. The combination of gesture and the imperative ensures both clarity and a brisk lively pace.

9. Don't commentate

It is essential to involve students in the learning process and discussion of classroom activities can often be valuable. Many inexperienced teachers, however, keep up a more or less non-stop commentary on their own activities.

> *Good morning everybody. Please sit down. Now this morning we're going to look at sentences like.... I'll put that on the board.... Oh dear, somebody hasn't cleaned the board .... Can anybody see the duster?.... Ah, there it is .... just a moment now. I'll just clean the board and then I'll put the example on the board for you* (cleans the board).... *Now, where was I? Ah, yes, now I'll just put the example on the board for you.*

There is another similar example which is very common:

> *Well, now we're going to read the text. I'll read it first and then I want you to read it after me and then there are some questions after the text and when we've read it I'm going to ask you the questions and you're going to answer them.*

Unfortunately, students never know whether what you are saying is important or not. Any commentary you give should be of help to the students, and not used either to reassure yourself or simply to fill up silence.

10. Don't be afraid of silence

Teachers, keen to encourage their students to talk, often forget that silence also has a valuable part to play in language lessons. *Constant* language is tiring; students need time to think, collect their thoughts, make notes, etc. Silence is particularly desirable:

a. When students are doing something individually — reading a text or explanation, completing an exercise, preparing a piece of work. If the teacher speaks during these activities, it breaks the students' concentration.

b. An individual is hesitating during an exercise, or looking for a word. Here, the teacher jumping in too soon makes the student lazy. The silent struggle to understand or recall is a natural part of language learning.

c. In discussions the student sometimes needs time to formulate a thought and, most important of all, if the teacher is constantly injecting ideas, students will soon sit back and *expect* the teacher to do the work.

d. Sometimes there should be silence for the sake of silence — if something hectic has been happening; there is to be a change of activity, or students need, for example, to get out a new book. A moment or two of silence in the middle of a lesson means that students can return with renewed concentration to the activity which follows.

Because the room is silent, it does not mean nothing is happening. The secret is a balance between activity and quiet moments for reflection.

11. Don't be afraid of noise

Many teachers particularly in state schools, may find colleagues and superiors who believe that the quiet class is the good class. Such a belief raises obvious difficulties if we are concerned to teach the spoken language!

If the standard teaching technique involves the teacher questioning individual students one by one, in every lesson no individual student will answer more than two or three questions, each lasting a few seconds. If the student has 120 lessons in a school year it is soon clear that each individual student will have only a matter of minutes for oral practice in any one year.

The conclusion is obvious — somehow or other, techniques must be used to increase the amount of student talking time. This means that anyone who is making a serious effort to teach oral English *must* be regularly using choral work, pair work and group work. Unfortunately, if 30 students speak at the same time they make more noise than is ever heard in the traditional question and answer classroom. The reason they make more noise is because there is more constructive activity going on!

Effective language teaching means giving the students a chance to speak. Carefully organised 'noise' does not mean disorder or that time is being wasted.

12. Use pair work to increase student talking time — even if it seems chaos

The language teacher must develop strategies for maximising the amount of student talking time. Well-organised pair work is one of the most important ways of achieving this.

To be "well-organised" the teacher must have given clear and explicit instructions and, while the pair work is taking place, the teacher should be moving around the room monitoring and if necessary guiding and correcting what individual pairs are doing. It may be necessary to write on the blackboard an outline or model of what the pairs should be doing or some key words and phrases.

After some time with the pairs working together, one or two pairs should be invited to 'demonstrate' and, if necessary, after pairs have demonstrated the teacher should add comments (both corrections of mistakes and suggestions for alternative, more natural, ways of saying things), then students should work in pairs again, possibly reversing roles.

Teachers worry that some of the pairs may not be doing the right thing, or will be using their native language. Because teachers are not satisfied that *everyone* is doing the correct thing, they are sometimes tempted to drop pair work. It is important to remember that if half the class are *not* doing the right thing, that still means half the class *are*! As a result, instead of one or two students doing something useful while the others sit back, 10 or 20 students are working constructively. Teachers must not drop pair work just because it is not successful for all students all the time. A moment's reflection will serve to remind teachers that when traditional question and answer lessons are taking place there is no guarantee that these are working successfully for most of the students — they may be sitting there quietly, but that doesn't mean everyone is working!

Your pair work will be most effective if you:

— Divide the group into pairs yourself and make sure that all students know who they are working with and which role they are to take.
— Make sure everyone is clear about what they are meant to be doing.
— Go round, listen, and check that they are doing it.
— Stop the activity when it is clear that everyone is finished. Pair work is not an excuse for the teacher to sit back!
— Follow up the pair work with a demonstration or summary from one or more pairs. If it is not well done, correct and provide help and then ask students to do the same practice again.
— Make a habit of it!

13. Use group work to increase student talking time

Many, if not most, activities in the language classroom can be performed by the students working in groups. Working in this way means more students are directly involved; more students are talking, while the teacher talks less; students can help each other; and not least, the atmosphere is more relaxed and conducive to good language learning.

Group work must be well organised which means the teacher must have made the task clear, as well as who is working with whom and for how long. Often it is a good idea to appoint one student in each group as "secretary" — writing out the answers,or taking notes to report back to the whole group. Group work must *always* be followed by a general class activity when the results of the group work are reported to the whole group, and commented on by the teacher.

Group work can be used as preparation for a text or topic; grammar practices can be done in groups rather than in the standard question-and-answer way; discussion follow-up can be based on questions first discussed in small groups, and later by the whole group.

As with pair work, some use of the native language is unimportant. It still means that the teacher, although busy moving from group to group, is relatively quiet, and many more *students* are using their English.

14. Be explicit

It is the teacher's task to structure classroom activities. This means planning in advance what is to be done and how it is to be done. It also means doing this *in detail.* If the teacher has only a woolly idea of what is required, the pace of the lesson will drop and students become either bored or confused.

Classroom instructions and explanations should be simple, precise, and explicit. A comment such as: *Verbs like see, hear, smell don't usually occur in the present continuous,* can easily be completely meaningless for the student. If the comment is a *reminder* of something which has been discussed earlier in the lesson or in the previous lesson it may be sufficient, but as an "explanation", it is not sufficiently explicit. If the explanation is to mean anything, the students need to understand in what way the verbs are similar; in some ways they are clearly dissimilar — phonetically, for example. Teachers sometimes say that it will take too long to give the full explanation or that it will confuse students. Such an argument does not justify giving vague explanations which require the students to do all the work of understanding, while the teacher avoids explaining.

More frequently than with explanation teachers give vague rather than explicit, instructions: *Can you work in pairs now please?* The following is not much better: *Work in pairs with the person next to you.* Unfortunately most people have at least two people next to them — one on each side! And what about the odd student in classes which have an odd number?

Written out in full the explicit instruction seems complicated, but in the classroom it probably takes only half a minute even with a large class, using your hands to indicate individual students:

Now you're going to work in pairs. Listen please, listen for your number, I'm going to give you a number, either 1 or 2. Make sure you know your number . . . 1,2; 1,2; 1,2; (pointing at individual pupils) *. . . Now, number ones, put your hand up please* (check) *and number twos* (check again).

If there is an odd student, ask that student to work with you then continue:

Now all the number ones I want you to . . . number twos, you . . . Right, altogether now, number ones — start!

Try such an explicit instruction with one of your larger classes — it takes only a few seconds with a class of 30 and is much more efficient than the confusion which often follows the apparently quicker *Work in pairs.*

Students like to know what is required of them. In asking students to work quietly, individually, or in pairs, give them a time limit. As the limit approaches ask *Are you ready?* and answer the chorus of *No!* by saying *Right, two more minutes, then.*

The more explicit your instructions, the easier it is for the students to concentrate on the content, rather than the organisation of activities.

15. Don't ask *"Do you understand?"*

The general question *Do you understand?* is usually either a sign of laziness on the part of the teacher, or something teachers say while thinking of what they really want to say. It may fill up a space, but that is all it does.

It is very rare indeed for students, particularly older students, to admit that they do not understand. Partly this is a natural desire to avoid appearing slow, but students also often unconsciously see another difficulty — if they say they do not understand they may be asked *what* they do not understand — and how do you explain what you don't understand? Part of being explicit involves the *teacher* checking whether students understand or not.

This is done first by keeping regular eye contact with the students while explaining. Often it is possible to see when students do not understand, and even to see the point at which they become lost or confused. It is also possible to tell whether the whole group, or only one or more individuals is confused. If it *is* necessary to ask, this should be done by asking specific questions about the information or explanation you have just given. The questions should require short, and linguistically simple answers. If students cannot answer the questions, they do not understand.

Jack's got a car but he used to have a motorbike.

Has he got a motorbike?
Has he ever had a motorbike?
What about now?

When giving the explicit instruction for pair work, we did not use *Do you understand?* but *Number ones put your hand up please.*
If anybody has not understood, it will be immediately apparent. It is then the teacher's job to anticipate difficulties and misunderstandings, and to make it as easy as possible for the students to show their difficulties without embarrassment.

16. Don't go 'round the class' if individuals can prepare particular examples

Usually, particularly in larger school classes, the students are sitting in carefully arranged rows. With certain types of practice, particularly textbook grammar practices, this means that if you follow the seating arrangement, individual students can prepare their 'own' example in advance. More importantly, it frequently means that students do not listen to the other examples! Obviously, you avoid this by choosing individuals to answer randomly rather than following a set pattern.

With some types of work, however, it is quicker and easier to do the practices in a simple pattern such as round the class, across rows or down lines of students. This will be true, for example, of an individual pronunciation practice of a word or phrase, or of certain types of language game. The guiding principle is simple: if the student is more likely to be able to 'switch off' if you follow a pattern, then you *choose* individuals to answer; if the emphasis is on speed and students will remain involved because of the pace, it is often more efficient to do things in an "obvious" way.

17. Admit your ignorance

No teacher can know everything and there is no harm in students recognising this. English is a huge subject and, no matter how much you have studied it, no matter how long you have been teaching it, you will still come across points which have never arisen before.

Native teachers have often not thought of some of the difficulties which foreign students face when seeing English " from outside ". Non-native teachers living in their own countries often do not have the opportunities to develop as wide a knowledge of English as they would like. It is extremely important for teachers not to feel guilty about this. State schoolteachers should think of teachers of other subjects such as mathematics or physics — it would be impossible for teachers in these subjects to know everything about their subjects; the same is true for English.

It is, on the other hand, important not to undermine the students' confidence in the teacher. The solution is straightforward — admit that you do not know, consult a colleague or look the answer up, and make sure that if you say you will tell the student in the next lesson, you do actually say something about the problem — even if you can't find the answer!

The worst thing to do is to give an *ad hoc* explanation which later turns out to be untrue. The best thing to do, in this as in so many other things, is to take the students into your confidence — do your best to help them, but if there are occasions when you cannot, make that, and the reasons for it, clear to them.

18. Consult colleagues

One of the quickest and easiest ways of finding the answer to a question which you cannot answer is to ask someone else. Why waste a long time wrestling with a problem, or wading through a reference book if a colleague can tell you in a few moments?

It is particularly the case that non-native teachers frequently have a better explicit knowledge of the grammar of English than an inexperienced native teacher has. In such circumstances it is common sense to pool your skills and make life easier for both of you.

Many non-native teachers working in state schools do not have regular access to a native speaker. They can, however, relatively easily form self-help groups. Teachers with different backgrounds have different insights and skills. At the same time most teachers teaching similar classes face similar problems. In these circumstances, teachers should get together, either informally or formally, on a regular basis. At least it helps to share problems, and to realise that others too find the tape difficult to hear, the distinction between the present perfect and past simple difficult to explain etc.

Often, however, such self-help groups can be significantly more useful than that. Because of the varied background of their participants, a combination of the insights of several group members can often produce a solution which no individual member would produce alone. One of the main reasons teachers resist the formation of such groups is, unfortunately, a false sense of their own importance. They are afraid that others will be unsympathetic to their difficulties, lack of knowledge, or other problems. While some ideas will work for individual teachers but not for others, it is astonishing how much collective wisdom is wasted by *not* being shared with colleagues. Such help can cover many fields — simple misprints in the textbook, convenient ways of explaining things which students have found difficult, useful supplementary practices, test items, sources of useful authentic material, etc. Teachers in many parts of the world have found such groups enormously helpful. Initially, people may be shy about raising individual difficulties and it is often best to begin such groups by having a task such as the preparation of a test or supplementary material for a difficult point, as the basis for an early meeting.

There is a saying *A trouble shared, is a trouble halved;* it is as true for the language teacher as for anybody else!

19. Consult students

Are some of your lessons better than others? If you have answered *Yes,* two more questions arise: *Why? How do you know?*

Every teacher thinks some lessons are more successful than others — perhaps you prefer one kind of activity to another, perhaps you hate teaching one particular grammar point which you know always causes trouble, or perhaps you find a particular group difficult or, as every teacher recognises, it might just be a Friday! But what about the students? Do they enjoy all of your lessons equally? Are there some activities they hate, and others they particularly enjoy? In state schools, it may be that they are not particularly tired on Fridays, but are always tired on Tuesdays, after maths, chemistry, and double physics!

As teachers we too often pretend that we *know* what our students feel, when it is extremely easy to find out by simply asking them.

Teachers spend a lot of time 'judging' students — either giving formal marks, or approving or disapproving of their performance. In these circumstances it should not appear so very shocking that perhaps occasionally students can be invited to judge their teachers or teaching! Why not, from time to time, ask your class:

> Did you particularly enjoy today's lesson? Why / Why not? What activities in your English lessons do you particularly like/dislike? What activities do you think we spend too much/too little time on in English classes?

Some activities can be done in different ways — why not ask students which ways they prefer, and which ways they don't like.

Remember, too, to ask students about the practical difficulties — Can they always hear you or the tape recorder? Can they see the blackboard? Can they read your writing? It is easy to see any negative responses as personal criticism and to react negatively. That would make the whole exercise useless. There is a danger in consulting the students too frequently, so that they feel the process of language learning is more important that learning itself. Providing, however, that you take the students' comments seriously, and do not do it too frequently, consulting students can have a very beneficial effect on the general atmosphere of your class, and sometimes reveal concrete ways in which your classes can be made more enjoyable or more effective for that particular group of students.

20. Demonstrate, rather than explain, new activities

A lot of class time is wasted if students do not know exactly what is expected of them. On the other hand, many activities occur again and again, so that time spent establishing a pattern for activities the first time they occur is repaid later.

There is no better, or more explicit, way to introduce new activities than for the teacher to demonstrate, or ask a group of students to demonstrate.

In cases where, for example, a question and answer pattern is to be passed from student to student down the lines of the desks in the classroom it is best for the teacher first to explain, and then ask *one* line to demonstrate. This means problems and misunderstandings can be sorted out before the whole class goes wrong and things become extremely confused.

Demonstrating reduces the amount of unnecessary teacher language, is explicit, gives an idea of timing, and is generally more effective than any explanation.

21. Exploit real events

Inevitably much of the language used in the classroom is unnatural — the teacher sets up situations and gives students an opportunity to practise. Unfortunately, opportunities for *natural* language use are often ignored.

Firstly, teachers should try to use natural language themselves, and occasionally draw attention to such uses as:

> *Sorry, I'm late . . . I'm afraid . . .*
> *Could you . . . please?*
> *Would you . . . please?*

If you sneeze, say *Excuse me;* if you know it is a student's birthday, say *Many Happy Returns;* in the first lesson of the spring term start by saying *Happy New Year.* It is better to present these expressions in natural contexts rather than coldly, as items to be learned.

More difficult, and more useful, is to stimulate the students into using the language naturally. Much modern material is based on the 'information gap' — a situation where two students each have different sets of information. Such situations do, however, arise naturally in the classroom — particularly, perhaps, between the native speaker and non-native student, but also for the non-native teacher in school classes when, for example, the students know something about school life which you have not yet heard. Such situations provide a real opportunity for students to use their English naturally and communicatively. For such an activity to be convincing it is not essential that the teacher *really* does not know the information; what is essential is that the students believe the teacher does *not* know, and genuinely *wants* to know.

Too often teachers try to *give* things to students. Some of the most lively and natural language use can be stimulated by *asking* students about what *they* already know, and are interested in.

22. Divide the blackboard

The reader is invited to stand at the back of his or her next class after the students have left and look at the blackboard with one question in mind — *Would what you can see help anybody?*

The blackboard is a visual aid; aids are supposed to help. A muddled, cluttered, mish-mash will help nobody.

Larger boards should be divided into three parts — two smaller side panels, and a larger central area. One side panel is used for listing new words and phrases, and is not cleaned during the lesson. Nothing else is put in this section. If the section is full, there is enough new material anyway in that lesson! (This section is even better replaced by a large pad of paper beside the blackboard on which a permanent record may be kept.)

The second small section is used for doodles, drawings, unexpected odds and ends etc. It may be cleaned constantly.

A large central section is used to present the main material of the lesson — grammatical examples, examples for exercises, etc. This may also be cleaned as required.

Try dividing your blackboard — it is a discipline which helps all teachers.

23. Use the overhead projector to control what students see

One piece of machinery is frequently available to language teachers but is under-used because they are not sure of its advantages — the overhead projector. Its advantages include:

— it is easier to write on a transparency than on the blackboard
— the transparencies can be prepared in advance
— important transparencies can be re-used, with different classes, or from day-to-day with the same class
— the teacher can build up a file of transparencies giving frequently needed exercises and clear, well-prepared examples for the most common grammar points.

An important point will be noted — in thinking about the slide projector one automatically thinks of projecting pictures; similar large coloured pictures do exist for use with the overhead projector but the advantages of the overhead projector are most obvious when it is used with transparencies of words — examples, exercises, and even dialogues and texts.

One very important warning is necessary. As most teachers who have seen the projector used in lectures will know, it is extremely annoying to be asked to look at a projected transparency where the text is too small for you to read. If you are going to use a transparency check what size of hand-writing you need to use to make sure it is visible to every student in the room. If you are using a typewriter it will be necessary either to use a special large-faced typewriter, or to blow the text up on an enlarging photocopier. Aids are only aids if they help!

The most important advantage of the projector, however, is that the transparency can be revealed slowly. Material which you prepare and write on the blackboard before the lesson is either open for all to see, or perhaps covered by a screen. When you remove the screen, all is visible. If you write on the blackboard during the lesson it takes a lot of time. The projector avoids both of these disadvantages. The material can be prepared in advance, and revealed at exactly the speed you wish to go at. A piece of paper placed over the projector can be easily manipulated while still looking at and talking to the class. This ensures that everybody is looking at the same piece of material. Two pieces of paper can be very simply used to provide a mask revealing the corners, lines, or columns of a prepared transparency.

With the blackboard, and even with a textbook, the teacher can never be sure what the students are looking at. With the projector you can control precisely what the students can see.

24. Machinery will not solve all your problems

Some years ago very large amounts of money were invested in language laboratories. Only after schools had invested their money, and students had been subjected to the laboratories, did it occur to people to ask whether there were enough good tapes available to justify the laboratory, and to think about the theory of how and why the laboratory could be helpful. In fact, the laboratory usually plays a very small part in most modern language courses (although the classroom tape is often very important).

The modern well-equipped language classroom of course needs a blackboard (divided into parts!), ideally a large block of paper beside the blackboard on which the teacher can write material which will be needed from lesson to lesson, a tape recorder, and, for the reasons we have just discussed, an overhead projector. Each of these has a valuable role to play and they all have something in common — the teacher remains in control of when and how they are used.

It is fashionable to talk about using video and computers in language teaching. Good use of these machines depends not only on the hardware, but on good software and on teachers being aware of the full potential of the machinery.

If you, or your school, are contemplating buying such machines it is usually wiser to *start* by buying an up-to-date book discussing the potential of the machine. If the software is available, and if you can integrate the use of the machine into your overall teaching programme, it will help. Unless, however, such work is a fully integrated part of your complete teaching programme there is a danger of wasting both time and money.

Machinery cannot do the work for you. It is only a first step. The second step is the software used on the machines and the third, and probably most important step is you, the teacher. No machine can smile at the student. Teaching is a personal activity and anything which obscures that needs to be treated with the greatest caution.

25. Expand, don't clutter

The greatest terror of the new, or less experienced teacher is that they might 'run out of material'. Horror of horrors — imagine standing up in front of a group of people with no plan, no material, and no idea what to do next! Strangely enough, if you are a well-balanced person, interested in other people, it will not turn out to be the problem you expect — indeed it can be the making of some people as teachers.

Less experienced teachers tend to take in material — piles of it — carefully, but all too often **over**-prepared. They are ready to teach some material, which all too easily becomes a barrier between them and the students. Bad teachers are disorganised — good teachers are organised — but very good teachers are half organised — and have the techniques at their disposal to develop a small amount of material in ways which respond to the student's particular needs or mood in that particular lesson. This book is specifically about techniques — how to do a pronunciation practice on the basis of any mistake; how to ask comprehension questions and conversation questions about any type of text; how to develop a simple collocation practice or drill a particular grammar point. Once you have mastered these techniques, you need relatively little material — it cannot be emphasised too much that you need a **small** amount of material which provides the basis of the lesson, and a **range of techniques** which allows you to develop that material in interesting, varied and effective ways.

Less experienced teachers are advised as strongly as possible to equip themselves with a range of techniques — which can be applied to different materials on different days in slightly different ways, and a range of activities or 'fillers' which provide an insurance policy, and the possibility of variety. Once you have these at your disposal, you will soon develop the confidence to take in only basic materials which you can then expand.

If you ever find yourself saying *I think we've just got time for a grammar practice/pronunciation practice/... before the end of the lesson* you have not taken on board the advice of this section — relax, stop pushing, create space. Remember, students learn best when they are relaxed; similarly teachers teach best when they are prepared and alert, but equally are also relaxed.

Chapter 4

Preparation

Mark each of these statements before and after you read the chapter.
Mark each statement

      ✔ if you *agree*.
      X if you *disagree*.
      ? if you are *undecided*.

1. You have to read the *whole* course book before you teach the first lesson.	
2. It is best to follow the order and pace of the course book.	
3. Over-prepared lessons are as bad as under-prepared lessons.	
4. Every lesson needs a short introduction.	
5. Every lesson needs a short summary at the end.	

Preparation

1. Prepare yourself

Nothing is more certain to guarantee a disastrous lesson than an unprepared teacher. Of course, all experienced teachers learn to provide fill-in lessons when someone is ill (or when they have forgotten to prepare!) and every teacher has given the occasional wonderfully successful spontaneous and unprepared lesson. In general, however, success is directly proportional to the care of preparation. This preparation should be detailed:

a. Decide *what* you are going to teach.
b. Make sure you have the necessary materials — books, tapes, pictures, etc.
c. Check the practical details — Have you enough copies of a stencil? Does the tape recorder work?
d. If you are going to use machinery, for example, the tape recorder, make sure the tape is in the right position *before* the class arrives (or, if this is impossible) before you start teaching.
e. Of particular importance is preparing any textbook material you intend to use. It is no good reading only the teachers' notes — you need to have looked at the material in the students' book *in detail*:

Have you checked the order you are going to teach the material?
Do all of the examples in the exercise fit?
Which words in the text will need explanation?
Which words in the text will need choral pronunciation?

In preparing a text for intensive reading it can be helpful to use coloured pens — one colour to underline new lexical items, one for items to be used for choral pronunciation, and one for items to be used as examples of the important structures practised later in the unit. The textbook is there to help you — but it can only do this if you have prepared the material adequately in advance.
f. The well-prepared teacher always has two or three "five-minute filler" items prepared so that if there are a few minutes at the end of the class the teacher has something *useful* and *different* to fill the gap.

2. Courses and lessons need an overall structure

Teachers frequently do not distinguish between long and short-term preparation. Long-term preparation is thinking about general course objectives which may include:
Why are these students studying English?

To what use(s) will they put it?
What kind of attitude will they bring to the subject?
How do the English lessons relate to the students' other activities? (both for adults or those studying in a state school setting)
Are students preparing for an exam? — if so, what is the *detailed* syllabus?

Of course all teachers pay lip service to these general course objectives, but it is necessary from time to time to stop, sit down, and think about how what you are doing in the classroom relates to the students' wants and needs. Very few courses, for example, include elements which help students to learn how to study languages better and yet many students will need to continue studying English without access to a teacher. Although note-taking and study-skills may not be required by the students for an exam for which they are preparing, they may well need these skills after they have succeeded in the exam. As we pointed out in the introductory chapter, language learning is more important than language teaching. This means it is essential for teachers to think about long-term objectives of any course. Almost invariably it is helpful if teachers working in a similar setting discuss from time to time how their courses relate to their students' needs.

Long-term preparation in the use of a textbook means reading and understanding the teachers' guide to it and reading all of the textbook *before* starting the course. Most modern textbooks re-cycle grammar and vocabulary or present the same language item from two different points of view, perhaps structurally and functionally, in different units. It is essential that teachers know when presenting a point for the first time that the point recurs several units later. The textbook may be a voyage of discovery for the class, but most certainly should not be so for the teacher!

Materials cannot be used effectively unless the teacher and author are working in harmony. The teacher needs to understand the rationale behind different activities of the book — is this particular activity aimed at accuracy or fluency? Or is a certain language item intended for the students' active or passive knowledge? In what ways does the author expect a teacher to supplement the book?

Almost always it is desirable for the teacher to adapt, supplement, or omit items from the textbook for a particular class. This can only be done, however, after the teacher understands how the individual elements of the course book fit into the author's overall plan.

3. Don't let the book dictate

It is very rare for a teacher to be completely happy with any textbook. A particular feature of the book may be inappropriate to the situation in which you are using it or there may simply be a feature of the book you dislike. It may not, however, be your decision whether that particular book is used or not. If you have to use a book which has features you dislike, it may help to make your disagreement clear to the students if, for example, you are going to omit practices of a certain type, but criticism of detail that could affect students' confidence in the book should always be avoided. It is sensible to tell students *before* you do a particular exercise that you are going to miss out a particular example. However, if it is clear to students that you and the book are going in different directions, they will be confused and their learning impeded.

At the same time the book should not dictate. We have already observed in the introductory chapter that you should teach students, not books.

Do not be afraid to change the order of the material presented in the book, omit particular items, or supplement the book by providing additional practice, or practices of a different kind. Such changes must, however, be planned in advance. The best lessons will usually be those in which the teacher uses the book as a support for a course which is centred on the students' needs.

4. Do not prepare too much or too rigidly

Inexperienced teachers frequently over-prepare. They worry about "drying-up" and, consequently, write out all their comprehension questions in advance, and plan in detail how long they expect each activity to take. While such planning can be helpful before the class, it is usually disastrous if taken into the classroom.

A lesson in which the teacher is pre-occupied with a lesson plan and more busy looking at the plan than at the students will be uninvolving and dull. A plan helps — but it should be a general framework, not a straight-jacket. There must always be opportunities for students to ask unexpected and awkward questions; the teacher should constantly be looking for opportunities to capitalise on the students' interest and on particular difficulties which emerge during the lesson. There is no merit in sticking to a plan for the sake of a plan — the plan is supposed to help the students; as soon as it stops doing that, it should be ignored.

Teachers find it helpful as part of their lesson preparation to make written lesson plans. In doing this it is important to remember that that plan will be used in the classroom. Usually you will be standing up or even moving around the room. Most often you will have a textbook in one hand and may well be using the other hand to encourage students, invite choral pronunciation, etc. A lesson plan written out on several sheets of paper will be impossible to use and will obstruct rather than help the lesson.

There is no harm in writing an extensive lesson plan, *providing* you then reduce it to a single page of clearly written headings, perhaps with page or tape references, which you will actually be able to use in the classroom in the hurly-burly of a lesson.

Once in the classroom, put the notes somewhere you can see them without inconvenience and, if you are going to look at them, do not attempt to keep this a secret. It is usually best simply to say *Excuse me a moment, I want to look at my notes.* Students expect you to be prepared, so there is no need to make a secret of your preparations. Lesson notes do help, providing they are *notes.*

5. Preparation must be concrete

There are many reasons why students may be unable or unwilling to contribute to a discussion or conversation in the language classroom. They may know nothing about the topic, or not be interested in it; they may not have the language to say what they wish; they may care deeply about the topic, and know they are unable to express their ideas with sufficient subtlety, so they prefer silence or a non-commital *It's difficult to say.*

The difficulty may, however, be simpler — students have simply not collected their thoughts and, while the teacher has thought about the topic, and is full of ideas, the students are still trying to adjust to the fact that the chemistry lesson has finished, and the English lesson has started.

Concrete preparation of the topic helps overcome some of the difficulties. Useful techniques involve the use of positive/negative tables, best/worst questions, and word-ladders and word-roses. These techniques take only a few minutes at the beginning of the lesson, and help to focus students' thoughts both on the ideas and language that may be needed to discuss a particular topic.

Positive/negative

Students are asked to write down three positive ideas, and three negative ideas, which they associate with a particular question, e.g. living in a town, a holiday in America, going to university, being unemployed.

The last example is important — most students would say that being unemployed is a bad thing, and would have little difficulty thinking of negative ideas associated with it, but some might say that there is another side to that as to most other questions. By using the positive/negative technique, students are encouraged to think widely and imaginatively, but at the same time concretely, about a question.

Best/Worst

Again, the idea is to encourage a wide spectrum of concrete ideas. What was your best/worst subject at school? What is the best/worst film you have ever seen? Who is your favourite/unfavourite relative? What food do you particularly like/hate?

Encouraging students to think in this way combines positive and negative ideas and means there is almost certain to be a width of opinion to any idea introduced into the conversation.

Word ladders and word roses

These are mentioned (page 108) to focus attention on vocabulary before reading a text. They are equally useful for focusing students' attention on vocabulary before a discussion or conversation.

In general, a few minutes concrete preparation at the beginning of "a conversation lesson", will be rewarded by a livelier discussion, with more participants, and a greater range of ideas.

6. Aids are only aids if they help

Flash cards, tapes, slides, pictures, wall-charts, video recordings and even textbooks themselves are there to help the teacher. They are not intended to replace the teacher. But neither are they intended to be used for the sake of it.

There is no point in drawing a picture, if the students already know what the word means. There is no point playing a tape unless it adds something to the lesson.

Some teachers think that audio-visual aids will make their lesson more interesting. That is true providing the aids are clearly integrated into the teacher's overall plan and contribute to that plan. Aids used for the sake of it tend to confuse and irritate students.

Teachers frequently forget that the most important visual aid in most classrooms is the blackboard. If this is to be an aid it must not be a confused muddle of careless writing, words written in odd corners and doodles! You are most likely to use the blackboard well (i.e. so that it helps your students) if you structure it (see page 52), but, even so, it is necessary to prepare model sentences and similar important blackboard material *before* the class.

If you are going to use a piece of mechanical apparatus it has to be pre-pared so that when you need it you can switch on and it works, immediately. If you use class time to thread a film or more commonly try to find the right place on a tape (particularly on a cassette machine which doesn't have a counter!) you will wish you had never taken your 'teaching aid' into the classroom. You will look incompetent and feel silly.

Preparation means plugging the machine in, making sure the tape is at the right speed, the right volume, is audible all over the room, and is in the right place to start. Aids help if, and only if, they have been prepared by the teacher.

7. Never ignore the practical difficulties

As far as possible, the teacher should be conscious of each and every student as an individual. Unfortunately very large classes in very difficult circum-stances often mean that this ideal is a long way from attainable. But teachers can, even in the most difficult circumstances, try to check that the *practical* details do not make it more difficult for any student than it needs to be:

> Can all the students hear you? (If you can't hear me, put your hand up!)
> Can they all hear the tape recorder?
> Can they all see the blackboard?
> Can they all see you, and in particular your hands and your mouth?
> Have they all got a copy of the text — or, if they are sharing, are you sure everyone can see a copy clearly enough to use it?
> Has everyone got paper and a pen or pencil?
> Does *everyone* know what he is expected to do during the next activity?

Each individual matters all the time — if you move to a point in the classroom where one student cannot see your mouth during a pronunciation practice, that particular student can influence the success or failure of that part of the lesson more than all the students who can see. As far as possible there should never be an individual thinking, or mumbling, *What about me?*

8. A good lesson has a beginning, a middle, and an end

This does not mean you need a complicated three-part lesson plan but too often teachers expect students to start 'cold' and finish the lesson for no other reason than that the bell has gone.

It is wise to begin most classes with a short introduction, reminding stu-dents of what happened last time and saying what you are going to study this time. Such an introduction may be only three or four sentences and should hardly ever be more than two or three minutes, but neither should it be omitted.

In the same way it is helpful for everyone at the end of a session (a lesson or a day's work) if it is rounded off neatly by the teacher providing a brief summary and perhaps telling students what will happen next time. Again, the summary should not be too long, but neither should it be omitted.

Chapter 5

Techniques — Listening

Mark each of these statements before and after you read the chapter.
Mark each statement

        ✔ if you *agree.*
        X if you *disagree.*
        ? if you are *undecided.*

1. Listening is a passive skill.	
2. Listening is a receptive skill.	
3. Students should never listen to a tape for more than two minutes.	
4. A tape of natural English confuses students.	
5. Listening is very important for elementary students.	

Techniques — Listening

1. Listening can be divided into sub-skills

Teachers recognise that speaking is a complex process and frequently correct students' mistakes in different areas — pronunciation, structure, stress, intonation. In the same way when students write, a wide variety of mistakes are noted and corrected. With the receptive skills — listening and reading, however, there is a tendency to use only general, global, questions. Like the productive skills, listening and reading can be sub-divided, so that it is not sufficient to ask, after students have listened to something, *Did you understand that?* nor even enough to follow up with a series of conventional comprehension questions. Listening is more complicated than that.

Among the sub-skills of listening are:
— ability to follow the *general* trend of what is said
— ability to understand *specific* details
— ability to *check* a specific piece of pre-knowledge against what is said
— ability to understand the speaker's *intention* (why did/(s)he say something?)
— ability to understand the speaker's *attitude* (how (s)he felt)
Students' listening skills will be improved more efficiently if teachers aim to teach sub-skills, as well as global listening comprehension.

2. Direct students' listening, particularly if it is taped

When using language outside the classroom, the user has many clues to help him or her to anticipate what will be said — the context, what was said earlier in the conversation, knowledge of the other participant(s) in the conversation, etc. It is artificially difficult to ask students to do listening practices without providing them with preparation which will allow them to use anticipation.

The amount of preparation which may be necessary varies according to the class, the level of difficulty of the material and the students' language level. It ought, however, always to include two elements — first, some kind of general, thematic introduction — the students should be told "what it is about"; secondly, they should be given some kind of guidance on the structure of what they are going to hear. This is done most effectively by giving them *two or three* questions in the correct order *before* they listen, so that the basic sequence of ideas mentioned in the passage is clear to them.

It may also be helpful to do vocabulary exercises, for example, asking students to call to mind words which are suggested by a particular topic; or even to provide examples of vocabulary or rhetorical devices which occur in the listening material. Listening materials should not be intended to trick students. Their listening is more likely to be more effective, and their listening skills developed more efficiently if their interest *and* linguistic expectations are aroused in advance.

3. Listening to a tape is difficult

Most teachers will readily recognise the difference between speaking a foreign language face-to-face with a native speaker, and speaking the same language on the telephone. Most people would agree that the second is considerably more difficult. There are many reasons for this — some to do with the technical changes in sound made by the machine, some much more straightforward — you cannot see the speaker's facial expression or watch lip movements and, most importantly of all, you cannot interrupt and ask for a repeat or clarification.

Listening to tape-recorded material, no matter how good the quality of the taping, shares all of these difficulties. Many students, including those who could converse reasonably effectively face-to-face, find extended listening to tape recordings extremely demanding. The warning for teachers is clear — first, the students' listening must be prepared; secondly, no students should be asked to listen for more than a very short period at one time. Two or three minutes is the maximum that students can listen to the tape before concentration wanders. For many students at lower levels the concentration span is to be measured in terms of 20 seconds and so-called listening practices which go on for long periods are a waste of everyone's time, and can be counter-productive.

4. Let students hear "the real thing" from early in their course

A moment's reflection reveals that when learning your mother-tongue you begin by listening. Foreign language teaching has usually been very different. Because it has been based on careful structural progression, and people rarely speak for more than a sentence or two using the same structure, listening has either not been taught, or been introduced relatively late in the course.

Most courses will benefit from the introduction of a little natural listening material at an early stage. Such material helps, providing teachers bear in mind, and make very clear to their students that they do *not* need to understand everything, and that there will be a *lot* that they will not understand. Providing teachers set elementary tasks based on the material (for example, given a set of instructions for how to find an unknown place, the task may be to decide only whether the *first* step is to turn left or right) — the fact that the speaker gives a great deal more information is not necessarily a bad thing. One of the skills of listening is to extract from a great deal of unwanted information a small piece of information which is of use to the listener.

As teachers increasingly understand that listening can be taught, rather than simply acquired, and that it can be divided into sub-skills, so they should be more willing to introduce *short* pieces of authentic listening into all courses at an early stage.

5. Make sure students can hear the difference between similar sounds

Students need to recognise differences before they can be expected to produce the difference themselves. The students' native language may perhaps not have one or other (or perhaps either) of the sounds /k/, /g/.

To test if they can hear the distinction, write a minimal pair containing the difference on the blackboard.

1	2
Cot	Got

and then give this instruction:

Listen, cot, cot (*pointing to the word on the board*) cot, cot . . .
Listen, got, got (*pointing to the word on the board*), got, got . . .
Listen again (*pointing to the appropriate word each time as you say it*) cot, cot, got, got, cot, got . . . . Look, (*pointing to the board*) cot is number one, cot, cot. Got is number two (*pointing*) got, got . . . Now I'll say one of the words. If I say this word (*pointing*) you say 1 . . . If I say this word (*pointing*) you say number 2 . . . Are you ready? Cot.

As the class call out (chorally) you can tell how many of the class can *hear* the distinction.

6. Use a variety of listen and respond activities

In real life we listen for only one reason — to understand a message. In language learning, we can listen for the message, but for many other things which will help the language learning process. Here are some things students can listen for:

Words and phrases which are understood but not familiar
Words and phrases that are familiar but not understood
A particular grammatical feature — personal pronoun, present continuous, expressions with *of* etc.
Words connected with a particular theme

In each case you could invite the students to respond non-verbally — by, for example, raising a hand — as they notice the feature they are listening for.

In addition, more imaginative responses can be called for by asking students who are listening to a dialogue to, for example:

Imagine where the speakers are/what they look like
Form a question they would like to ask one of the speakers
Note where they agree/disagree with one of the speakers
Imagine a continuation of the dialogue

You learn to speak by good listening; good listening means the listeners are actively involved. The teacher's task is to devise techniques which help students to be involved, and give you the opportunity to monitor involvement. You should have little difficulty in adding many alternatives to the short lists of 'things to listen for' presented here.

Chapter 6

Techniques — Speechwork

Mark each of these statements before and after you read the chapter.
Mark each statement
>✓ if you *agree.*
>X if you *disagree.*
>? if you are *undecided.*

1. Teachers should always speak at a natural speed.	
2. Choral pronunciation is useful for all classes.	
3. Students need to know phonetics.	
4. "I never say 'Good' about a student's pronunciation unless it *is* good".	
5. Students should learn RP pronunciation.	
6. Consistency is as important as accuracy for students' pronunciation.	
7. Stress and intonation are not important in beginners' courses.	
8. Stress, pitch and intonation are best shown with your hands.	
9. Stress is sometimes as important as grammar.	
10. Bad intonation can lead to important misunderstandings.	

Techniques — Speechwork

1. Do not distort when giving a model

Teachers frequently try too hard to help students with pronunciation — they slow down to such an extent when giving the model for the student to imitate that it is distorted. While few teachers would pronounce the last part of *comfortable* as if it were *table*, it is very common in other words to give the neutral vowel its full value instead of reducing its value. It is perhaps particularly common with the articles when first introducing new vocabulary. The teacher should remember to say

a book   /ə/ /b ʌ k/
the pen   / ðə / /pen/

and not the stressed equivalents.

In the stress patterns of normal speech weak forms and contractions occur frequently. The danger in slowing down is that weak forms will be stressed and contractions lengthened. If students have difficulty, for example, with a phrase like *they mustn't've* it is not helpful to slow this down to the point where it becomes *they must not have* which is totally unnatural.

Distortion usually results from speaking in a slow, exaggerated fashion. It is better to give students a model at natural speed, using natural pronunciation and, if necessary, repeat it several times, rather than slow down.

2. The model must remain the same

It is characteristic of natural language use that *exact* repetition (the same words, the same structure, the same stress pattern, and the same pronunciation) is extremely rare. The very act of repeating usually means that an alternative stress pattern is appropriate. When presenting a model for a student two or three times it is important for the teacher to maintain absolute consistency. This is particularly difficult in giving examples of stress or intonation. The best way to acquire the skill of being able to repeat the same sentence is practice but if you find it difficult to repeat the same sentence identically several times in quick succession, it is useful to remember that if you say something else between — a simple comment will do *(I'll say that again)* — it is easier to produce an identical repeat. The interpolated comment should be short enough to distract you, but not long enough to distract the students!

3. Use choral pronunciation

The technique of choral pronunciation, in which all the students of the class repeat simultaneously, is much under-used. Teachers feel they cannot do pronunciation with students who are not beginners, or that they cannot use it with particular classes because of the type of student involved. The technique is useful with *all* students, at all levels, and save for classes containing only two or three students, for all class sizes.

It is true that it is of particular use with larger classes, with younger students, and with students at lower levels. This does not mean, however, that it should not be used with other classes. It can also be a useful classroom technique even if its main objective is not always only improved pronunciation!

Choral pronunciation serves to bring the class together and to re-focus students' attention on the teacher after some activity where their attention has been elsewhere — perhaps private study of a text, or pair work. Instead of calling for the students' attention it is sufficient for the teacher to say something like *Let's say some of the new words and phrases.* The manner in which the choral pronunciation is done (see below) can ensure that the students' attention *is* focused on the teacher.

Because the teacher controls the speed of the choral pronunciation practices, it is a useful technique for the teacher who wishes to speed up a lesson and re-involve everybody after any activity which has "sagged".

The technique is useful not only in bringing a class together, but in taking the pressure off individuals. Many students, particularly at lower levels, are very self-conscious when asked to pronounce new language items. Experience tells them that there is a reasonable chance that they will get these wrong and that they may say something which sounds rather funny. A student who is relaxed is more likely to learn well than one who is tense and self-conscious. The implication is obvious — when new language items are introduced it is usually a good idea for the teacher to say these first and to invite the class as a whole to repeat. After this has been done, perhaps several times, the teacher can invite individuals to repeat the same items — the ideal solution is choral *and* individual pronunciation — CIP work.

Although called choral "pronunciation", the technique is equally suitable for providing a model for stress or intonation practices which the students repeat in a similar way. For this reason it is frequently useful for students who are more advanced or older than teachers would sometimes consider suitable for CIP work.

Well used, the technique is fun, lively, increases the pace of the lesson, helps individuals to relax, and is one of the principal techniques which enable teachers to create a pleasant, relaxed yet dynamic classroom.

4. Conduct choral pronunciation decisively

Usually the teacher gives the model then invites the class to repeat: *I'm afraid not — can you say that together, please.*

It is a mistake for the teacher to keep on repeating the model and, in particular, the teacher must not repeat the model *with* the students. If the teacher speaks simultaneously with the students, the only voice that the teacher will hear will be his or her own!

To avoid this it is easier to invite the students to speak, and "conduct" them using your hands. Choral pronunciation is fun, but it is also very effective for the teacher, *providing* the students do speak approximately simultaneously. This of course means that a *decisive* hand gesture is required. Teachers should experiment with their own gestures until they find one with which they feel comfortable.

It is frequently easier once a pattern has been set to use a simple verbal cue for further repetitions:

T	I'm afraid not — can you say that together, please, *(gesture)*
C	I'm afraid not
T	Again
C	I'm afraid not
T	Again
C	I'm afraid not

By using a *standard* verbal cue — *Again* — students are not confused. Verbal conducting is more effective than gesture, particularly if the teacher is moving around the room at the time.

5. Move around the room when doing choral pronunciation

If the students are speaking at the same time but the teacher stands in one place it is difficult to hear their mistakes. If the teacher moves around the room while the choral pronunciation is being repeated it is, even in large classes, possible to note which individual students are either not speaking, or need help with a particular problem. Particularly with school classes the teacher moving between the desks helps to keep the students' concentration on the teacher, keeps everyone involved, and ensures that the teacher notes the individuals who need help. It also helps to ensure that the individuals you ask after the choral repetition change from one practice to another as you inevitably tend to ask students near you.

6. Keep your language to a minimum in pronunciation practices

We have remarked that the teacher should not speak with the class when doing choral pronunciation; there are, however, other temptations. It is not necessary to comment verbally on the standard of pronunciation; a smile, or slight shake of the head is sufficient. In the latter case the teacher should, of course, provide a new model. In continuing to the individual stage of pronunciation it is not necessary to invite students by name to speak; again a gesture is sufficient and, rather than saying *Good*, or something longer, a smile and a nod, or a slight shake of the head followed by an immediate new model from the teacher to be repeated immediately by the student who made the mistake, is quick, efficient and amusing, and avoids inhibiting students.

The importance of choral pronunciation as a technique for changing the tempo of the lesson has already been emphasized. It will only do this if it is done briskly, *without* the teacher providing a commentary. The basic guideline is that once the teacher has given the basic model, everything else consists of the *students* speaking, either chorally or individually, with the teacher's contribution restricted to the use of hands and eyes and perhaps single 'control' words.

7. Vary your criterion of "good" in pronunciation practice

Pronunciation is, in fact, a relatively small part of the problem of learning a foreign langage. While it is true that a consistent accent is easier to listen to (and probably more socially prestigious), it is certainly neither necessary nor desirable that many learners should achieve native speaker pronunciation. It is also true that some students find pronunciation particularly difficult — they seem to find it difficult to hear distinctions clearly, and correspondingly difficult to mimic accurately. This does not necessarily mean that they will not be reasonably successful in other areas of language learning. It is obviously psychologically important not to discourage those who find pronunciation difficult in the early stages of learning. Teachers should beware, therefore, of setting an artificially high standard of correctness in the early stages, and, as different students progress at different rates, it is wise to accept different degrees of variation from the 'ideal' target. It will help nobody if particular students have their confidence undermined and are constantly being asked to repeat because their pronunciation is less good than the rest of the class. A positive atmosphere, an encouraging teacher, and time, will probably do more than over-insistent teacher correction.

The implication is that *Good* is to be used differently to different students; and differently at different stages of each student's learning.

8. Articulation is an important first step in practice

Presenting language to the students does not guarantee that they will be able to use it and, of course, what they are unable to pronounce is useless to them. Students will frequently need to practise the articulation of new language before moving on to more meaningful practices. To practise *if I were you I'd . . . .,* for example, begin with choral and individual pronunciation of a number of sentences using the structure:

If I were you I'd wait / phone her / ask him / do it / try.

Time spent here will be more than saved in later practices which will not need to be interrupted so often to correct pronunciation. The language should by then be sufficiently automatic that students can concentrate on the meaning in the later communicative practices.

9. It is helpful to do articulation practices more than once

Most language teaching now places a strong emphasis on a methodology which is "communicative". Teachers sometime think this invalidates purely mechanical or "meaningless" practices. Far from it! We need to remember that you cannot communicate anything at all unless you can say the words in a way which the hearer can understand. Part of language teaching, only a small part perhaps, but a part nonetheless, involves language as a motor activity. Pronunciation involves both knowledge — which can frequently be looked up in a good dictionary — *and* skill — the physical ability to articulate the sound. As anyone who has ever played a sport will know, movements which you have done often are usually relatively simple to repeat, while using muscles which you have not used before (or for a long time) can be difficult. The sounds of one language are often not identical with those of another;

the *combinations* of sounds which are possible in one language are not the same as are possible in another — in English, for example, consonant clusters (*str, spr, bl,*) are frequent while many of the clusters of English do not occur at all in, for example, Italian.

Practices which are particularly intended to practise a motor skill — here, the ability to articulate particular sounds or groups of sounds — will frequently be most effective if the students do them more than once — perhaps first rather haltingly, then immediately after, rather more fluently, then perhaps even a third time still in the same lesson. This, of course, assumes that the practice in question takes only two or three minutes so that, even if done three times it is still only a five-minute activity. In these cases it would probably be desirable to follow up by repeating the practice again in a subsequent lesson.

The ability to type does not come from knowing the keys and pressing them once; many hours of mechanical practice are necessary. Similarly, students need to repeat articulation practices several times in order to gain control over their pronunciation. If you explain why you are doing such practices again and if they are done briskly, no-one will mind. Students never resent and are never bored by practices which they see are helping them.

10. Bring variety to "Say after me"

We have just suggested that articulation practices may perhaps be done several times. Some readers may feel this is a recipe for boredom but, far from it, if the manner in which they are done is varied there is no reason why they should not be a positive and lively contribution to the lesson.

Pronunciation is much more than "Say after me". In real life we use language in a wide variety of ways on different occasions — sometimes we shout, sometimes we whisper. This can be introduced to the classroom — either with a simple pronunciation practice or a more complex articulation practice. If the students are to repeat more than once, they can be encouraged to speak normally the first time, to whisper the second, and to shout the third.

This is not just a light-hearted technique, there is clear evidence that when students forget *what* they are doing, and particularly in the case of younger school classes start to *enjoy* it, they will become less inhibited and will find pronunciation easier.

There are many other techniques for bringing variety to the simple "Say after me" teacher-model followed by CIP. The class can be divided into halves and speak alternately; into lines or rows which speak consecutively. With some more complicated pronunciation work pairs can ask and respond simultaneously, or consecutively.

Introducing variations into the groups who are speaking, and how they are speaking, means that "simple" pronunciation practice can become an effective classroom technique in improving both the students' language work and as an important element in the creation of an enjoyable atmosphere.

11. Something which is not a real word sometimes helps

Because of the authority usually given to the written, and in particular the printed, word, it is tempting to think that words on the page reflect accurately the way we speak. This is not the case. The "spaces" when we speak do not necessarily lie in the "spaces" betweeen written words. It is a characteristic of natural spoken English that a consonant at the end of one word will be "linked" to the beginning of the next word if that begins with a vowel sound: Not *news item,* but *new sitem.*

This is particularly important with unstressed pronouns and auxiliary verbs.

In normal educated speech an initial /h/ is not omitted on stressed words but on unstressed words initial /h/ is not usually pronounced. The result is that linking is very common in situations where unstressed pronouns and auxiliaries occur. Students will find it difficult to say:

He mustn't have done it

unless they understand that one 'bit' is /t ə v/. They will need to practise saying /t ə v/ although this is not a 'word' if they are ever to say *it mustn't have* naturally.

If students read they will inevitably break the flow of sounds in the wrong places and have corresponding difficulty in producing natural stress and intonation. Teachers can help by demonstrating appropriate "groups of sounds", which may not necessarily correspond to written words. This means pointing out to students, and encouraging them to say, for example, *napple, a napple.* It is particularly important in *He was there wasn't he* where if the students gives the vowel sound of *he* full value, and makes the break in the wrong place, there is no way they can produce the tag at all naturally. They will need to be encouraged to say the terminal sounds of that sentence as: *wasn tea.*

In *not yet,* the linking of the /t/ and /j/ sounds produces a sound similar to that at the beginning of *children.* Observation shows that almost all native speakers of English using the phrase *All right,* pronounce it as if it were spelt *or right.*

If teachers are to encourage natural production from students, they must not allow the *printed* word to dominate. Saying things which look and sound funny in isolation can, if linked to natural native speaker examples on tape, be both amusing and help students to be both better listeners and more natural speakers.

12. There is no such thing as "the c-h sound"

English spelling is frequently only loosely related to the sound and, accordingly, can easily cause confusion. Any serious learner of English will need to learn a system of phonetic transcription, not in order to transcribe, but in order to read pronunciation in a good dictionary.

Teachers frequently feel, however, that phonetics is an added confusion, especially with younger students, students at lower levels, and with those who find language learning difficult. While this may be true, it does not mean that teachers should then make misleading references. It may be helpful to be told that the sound in the middle of *Not yet* is "similar to the sound at the beginning of *church*". What is *not* helpful is to call it "a c-h sound", otherwise the student is very reasonably going to make mistakes which have been encouraged by the teacher when meeting words like *machine* and *chemistry.*

There are two solutions — to teach the students the very small number of symbols which are required for the sounds which they constantly get wrong.

This would mean them knowing only three or four phonetic symbols which could then, where necessary, be written on the board to support oral comments such as "like the sound at the beginning of *church*". The second solution is simply to refer verbally to an appropriate example of the sound and, of course, to isolate and demonstrate the sound itself.

13. The main criteria for pronunciation are consistency and intelligibility

There is something slightly absurd about learners spending hours perfecting "a standard accent". This does not, however, mean that pronunciation does not matter. It is extremely difficult to listen to a speaker whose pronunciation is inconsistent, and it is tiring to listen to one who varies considerably from standard. Bad pronunciation can be a serious block to communication. On the other hand there is no harm in a foreign speaker *sounding* foreign. Listeners are more likely to make allowances for the language and behaviour of someone they recognise as being a foreigner. Try to present a standard model for pronunciation and make sure that students' approximations of it are consistent and intelligible, but do not expect them to reproduce it exactly.

It is easy for a Spanish-speaking teacher teaching Spanish-speaking students to become so used to their way of speaking that the teacher forgets or does not notice that students are deviating so much from standard pronunciation that they will be difficult to understand for people who are not used to their particular English. It is not enough for you, who are used to your students, to understand them — they have to be comprehensible to strangers as well!

Do not set such a high standard for pronunciation that students cannot achieve it. It is particularly important that they are *consistent;* it is less important that they produce individual sounds in a standard (RP) accent. Too much attention should not be paid to the sounds; often wrong stress can make students more difficult to understand, or more tiring to listen to, than slight variations in the way they produce individual sounds.

14. Teach intonation by back-chaining

In most English sentences the pitch movement at the *end* of the sentence is important for meaning. Students frequently find it difficult to repeat long sentences after the tape or teacher. In this case the teacher should break the sentence down into bits and build up towards the complete sentence. Because of the importance of the intonation of the end of the sentence in English, it is usually better to begin to break the sentence down from the *end*, rather than the beginning.

The reader may check this quickly by counting aloud from 1 to 6. It will be noted that the voice falls significantly on **6**. If you now try to repeat the following sequence, *not* as independent units, but as part of the full sequence: *one, two, three, four, five, six;*

One, two
One, two, three
One, two, three, four
One, two, three, four, five
One, two, three, four, five, six.

it will be noted that it is extremely difficult. Beginning at the end, however, because the end remains consistent, the intermediate stages are relatively easy, and contribute towards the ability to produce a complete sequence. The reader should try this sequence:
Five, six.
Four, five, six.
etc.

As an example *Do you mind if I smoke?* could be back-chained as follows:

T	Smoke
C	Smoke
T	if I smoke
C	if I smoke
T	mind if I smoke
C	mind if I smoke
T	Do you mind if I smoke
C	Do you mind if I smoke

Beginning at the beginning means that the intermediate stages are not contributing naturally towards the final version; back-chaining overcomes this difficulty.

15. Don't explain intonation, demonstrate

Linguists have devised several systems for transcribing intonation and these are used in some textbooks. Many students, however, find understanding the transcriptions more difficult than the intonation itself !
     Although students may find intonation difficult, the teaching of intonation is usually most effective when the teacher uses the simplest methods of presentation. These involve giving an exaggerated model and indicating the pitch movements either by movements of the hand, or by simple arrow drawings on the blackboard.
     The principle is clear from the two different intonations of the single word *Sorry:*

     Sorry!(Apology)   **Sorry?**(Please repeat)
A simple gimmick to introduce the idea of the importance of intonation is to use the single word above, demonstrate the two forms and then use a visual symbol to suggest each — a hand behind the ear should prompt the student to say *Sorry?*, while a sharp movement of the elbow should prompt the student to say *Sorry!*
     But, while such gimmicks can be helpful in teaching individual intonation items, the basic method is an exaggerated presentation, accompanied by simple hand movements or *simple* arrow drawings.

Make use of words and phrases which the students can already pronounce to help with the intonation of new items rather than trying to explain. If, for example, students have difficulty in saying tags like *isn't it, doesn't he* with falling intonation, it will help to repeat a sequence such as

       holiday   *Saturday*   *isn't it.*

16. Show stress, pitch, and intonation visually

This extends the idea discussed above. Stress is shown by the teacher making a decisive downward gesture with a closed fist to indicate the stressed syllables; pitch is shown by an exaggerated *positioning* of the hands; intonation is shown by upward or downward *movements* of the hands.

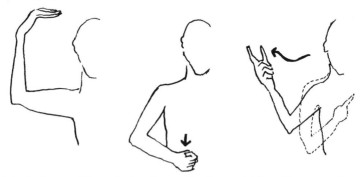

Such techniques, although simple, are for the majority of language learners, more effective (and more fun) than complex systems of written transcription.

17. Refer to stress and intonation even when not specifically teaching it

We have already seen that communication involves structure, stress, and purpose. Textbooks do not always reflect this. Most modern textbooks draw explicit attention to the fact that they teach certain structures, and certain functions (purposes). But unless the student has a reasonable control not only of pronunciation, but of stress and intonation, he will be both difficult to listen to, and easily misunderstood.

    For these reasons it is important that the teacher bears in mind that stress and intonation are important, even if doing comprehension questions after a text or the examples from a grammar practice. If students deliver the answers to the questions in a dull, monotonous or mechanical way, that is as much a "mistake" as a pronunciation or grammatical error and should come under consideration as one of the mistakes worth correcting.

    Language teaching is still strongly influenced by the feeling that the written word, in which stress and intonation play no part, is the objective for most students. Curiously, this attitude remains as a hidden ideal of many courses which are now based on taped material and have explicitly communicative aims. If students are to use the spoken language effectively, stress and intonation need to be given their real place in the teaching at *all* times.

    The impression people form of each other is frequently more dependent on intonation than grammar, and this should be a constant reminder of the important role it should play in teaching.

Chapter 7

Techniques — Structure

Mark each of these statements before and after you read the chapter.
Mark each statement
> ✔ if you *agree.*
> X if you *disagree.*
> ? if you are *undecided.*

1. Most grammar rules have exceptions.	
2. It is best to give a rule before you do a practice.	
3. Examples are more important than 'rules'.	
4. Knowing a rule does not mean you can *use* the language better.	
5. Students need to know terms like 'present perfect', 'imperative.' etc.	
6. The third person-*s* is not really very important!	
7. Fill-in exercises are best done orally.	
8. All students need both oral and written practices.	
9. Free practices are best omitted unless students do them well.	
10. Grammar will always be 'the boring bit' of a language course.	

Techniques — Structure

1. Encourage students to see patterns

There are long and complicated arguments about what learning a language really involves. But we can identify at least two different parts to the learning process:

a. The learning (memorising) of unrelated items — if I know the English word for 'cat', it will not help me in any way to learn the words for, for example, dog and horse. Unfortunately, much language learning is of this kind and often, even if we wish or hope for a pattern, there is none (for example *weather* is uncountable but *in all weathers* is a standard lexical item.)

b. A facility to use certain patterns of the language which are accepted as in some sense standard (and by implication an ability to avoid non-standard patterns).

Whenever the teacher can guide the student to the perception of a pattern, the learning load will be lighter. On the other hand, if the student is taught that something is the pattern which in fact is not so, he is likely to be unnecessarily confused. It is the job of textbook writers and teachers to try to draw attention to helpful patterns and, in the modern classroom in which the student is involved in his own learning, to help the student to discover the patterns for himself. Here are some simple examples:
If students are going to learn the verbs with irregular forms from a table, that table may, for example, be arranged alphabetically. Such an arrangement reveals no pattern at all and we may find next to each other:

Feel	Felt	Felt
Find	Found	Found
Fly	Flew	Flown
Forget	Forgot	Forgotten

However, there are phonological patterns which make learning easier so it must be a better idea to use a table which groups the verbs according to those patterns. In such a case, for example, this group occurs together:

Freeze	Froze	Frozen
Speak	Spoke	Spoken
Steal	Stole	Stolen
Weave	Wove	Woven

The responses to the following show a more complicated pattern:

A   Excuse me can you change a pound please?
B   I'm afraid I can't.

A   Excuse me, do you know what time the bank closes?
B   I'm afraid I don't.

A   Is there anything I can do about it?
B   I'm afraid there isn't.

It's tempting to draw attention to the pattern: *I'm afraid ...+ n't.*
But this is also possible:

A   I suppose you told Dick.
B   I'm afraid I did.
(It is also possible to say, with a different meaning *I'm afraid I didn't).*

An exception perhaps? — but what is the use of a pattern which is supposed to simplify the memory load if you also have to learn all the exceptions! In fact this is not an exception to the real, underlying pattern, only to the apparent pattern based on the first few examples.

(The real pattern in this case is that *I'm afraid* is added to a response which the speaker thinks his hearer (questioner) will interpret as being *semantically,* though not necessarily grammatically, negative — although we are not suggesting that it would ever be presented to a class in those words)

The ability to recognise items which are similar in some way will make it easier for the student to learn. Part of the teacher's job is to construct and draw attention to groups which make such similarities clear to students.

2. Good rules can help students

There have been times in language teaching when it was normal for the teacher to give a "rule", two or three examples, and the students went on to practise. At other times the process has been quite different — teachers have believed that stating rules confused students so that they have simply presented a larger group of examples, and then students have done practices. The sequence has been much discussed, as have the rules themselves. An understanding of the nature of language rules helps teachers and students. A few teachers still believe in *prescriptive* rules — rules which tell us what "should" and "should not" be possible in the language. This is a mistake. All linguists believe rules should be *descriptive* — they should say how the language *is* used, not how it *should* be used.

In a similar way all linguists are agreed that it is not sufficient to divide language into "right" and "wrong"; language is more complicated than that. Full, accurate descriptive rules will need to describe language as standard/ non-standard, appropriate/inappropriate, spoken/written, formal/informal, etc. For many students some of these distinctions are too complicated and too subtle, but for language *teachers,* all are always important.

For the descriptive linguist the important feature of a rule is that it is an accurate description; the description may be long, complicated,and need technical terms. For the language teacher a compromise needs to be made between the *accuracy* of the rule, and its *accessibility.* In short, a rule which is perfectly accurate but which students cannot understand is no help to them. Equally important, however, is that a rule which is inaccurate, even if the students can understand it, will often at a later stage in learning lead to confusion.

Very often language teachers are so anxious that the student will understand the 'rule' that they lean towards accessibility at the expense of accuracy. Many teachers, for example, teach the 'rule':

> **Some** in positives
> **Any** in negatives and questions

Such a rule is nonsense as the following examples show:

> I *like some* pop music.
> I *don't like some* pop music.
> I *like any* pop music.
> I *don't like any* pop music.

What justification can there be for introducing a 'rule' which is totally inaccurate? The teacher who uses that rule is forced to select examples which fit it and ignore examples which do not. The teacher then also has to hope that no student in the class will introduce an *Ah, yes, but it says here ...* example!

What is the clue to the use of good rules? It is first important to understand that the rule is not just a brief verbal description. The rule is a *combination* of a wide range of natural examples, verbal description, and, perhaps most importantly of all, the *relationship* between the verbalisation and the examples. This may make it sound complicated and, in one sense, it is. We have already observed that language is a system and that one element of language learning involves understanding the system; we have also noted that language learning is cyclical. Teachers must recognise this, and encourage an understanding of it in their students.

Too often, course books and teachers adopt a catalogue approach — students learn "a particular use" of, for example, the present simple, then "another use", and, in a similar way, several "uses" of the present continuous. At no point do they sit down to examine *the* fundamental difference between the two forms. That difference is one of the most important characteristics of English as a system and is a difficult problem for most foreign learners of English. It is not, however, an impossible problem, and, if approached sensibly, no more difficult than learning more and more apparently separate non-systematic "uses".

Natural examples help students to see how the language is used; good verbal descriptions help students to understand the significance of particular points of usage. The examples support the explanation, the explanation supports the examples. Understanding the rule is a *process,* in which understanding is deepened through re-cycling examples and explanation.

There are pitfalls which it is important for the teacher to avoid — the examples must not be chosen to fit the explanation; the explanation must not be "simplified" to the point that it is either meaningless, or hopelessly inaccurate. Some students will benefit particularly from examples, others will find descriptive explanation more useful. *Both* are needed if everybody is to be given the maximum possible help.

Teachers are sometimes heard to say *I don't give rules. They just confuse my students.* This is cheating. If the teacher gives examples and expects the students to infer or deduce the rules themselves, that must be more difficult than having access to a well-formulated verbalisation of the explanation. It may be true to say that giving students the rule highlights their misunderstanding, but it does not create it. The principle is that *good* rules help students — where 'good' means a compromise between accuracy and accessibility, and where 'rule' is a combination of cyclically presented well-chosen examples and verbal description.

(Several language points which are often mis-understood are discussed in Chapter 12).

3. Understanding involves example, explanation, and practice

At different times structure has been taught in very different ways. One school of thought believed that if students were given a "rule" they could then do examples which followed the rule; in reaction to this, a method evolved whereby students were given a group of examples, were expected to see what those examples had in common themselves, and were then required to produce other similar examples. Arguments have raged about whether to explain before, during, or after presenting examples and so on. All such arguments are unnecessary. Any solution which suggests that one method is likely to succeed when another fails is almost certainly misleading and an over-simplification.

Sometimes a pattern quickly emerges from examples:

A Have you ... ?   **A Can** you ... ?
B No, I **haven't**.   **B** No, I **can't**

The examples reveal the structure of B's response. Little explanation is necessary.

Sometimes, partly because of the language itself, and partly perhaps because of mistaken ideas introduced in the student's earlier learning, explicit explanation may be much more important. Many students believe, for example, that there are two quite different kinds of question in English — questions with (**do**), and questions without (**do**). If the former are taught first, the latter are "exceptions". In fact, all questions follow the same pattern and the explicit statement of a rule may help students to see this:

> **To make a question invert the order of the subject and first auxiliary; if there is no auxiliary introduce (do) as a "dummy" auxiliary, and follow the basic rule.**

The example illustrates the problem — the rule alone does not help the student, and examples alone make it difficult for the student to find the rule.

Understanding is a cycle which involves each of explicit explanation, example, and practice. Each part of the cycle contributes in its own way to understanding. It is not sufficient for students to understand intellectually; what students "understand" should directly influence their language performance. This is best achieved if teachers constantly bear in mind the important link between explanation, example, and practice.

4. Terminology can help or hinder

Students learning a foreign language will need either an explicit or implicit understanding of the categories and patterns. Teachers will frequently wish to refer to these patterns and will need a shorthand way to do this — some sort of terminology is inevitable.

Few teachers would doubt that it is practical for teacher and student to understand terms like *noun, verb, adverb, auxiliary.* Very often, however, these terms are used *without* making sure that students do genuinely understand them. While introducing the terms early in the students' course, teachers should plan to make their explanation and understanding part of the lesson, rather than an aside from the teaching of a structure.

Terminology can confuse as much as help — particularly if it is not introduced as a deliberate part of the teaching programme. English nouns divide into *countable* and *uncountable* ; countable nouns then divide into *singulars* and *plurals.* Singulars refer to *one* thing; *plurals* refer to *more than one* thing; both singulars and plurals refer to things which are, in English, *conceptualised in units.* Uncountable nouns refer to things which are *not* conceptualised in units *(weather, music)* — they are neither singular, nor plural. Uncountable nouns, however, do take singular verbs (Music *helps* me to relax).

It is not a matter that certain nouns are countable and others uncountable; certain *meanings* of a particular word are countable (*A cheese* fell on his foot); while other meanings of the same word are uncountable *(Cheese* is good for you).

This is a complicated idea for students. As already discussed, understanding involves a statement of the rule, examples, and practice. Any clear statement of the rule will involve introducing the terms *countable* and *uncountable,*but introducing the terms will only help if time is taken to ensure that students understand the categories to which they relate. The names themselves are somewhat unsatisfactory — one thing which we count in real life is money, but the noun *money* is uncountable. If the normal terms are used, teachers must be aware of the potential confusion introduced by the terminology. If alternative terms are chosen (*unit nouns, non-unit nouns*), while these may be more accurate and helpful, students will have to learn to relate this terminology to the standard terminology of text and reference books.

Teachers need to approach the problem stage by stage. First, give examples of a grammatical category, and then introduce the name. Check that students understand the name by asking students to sort examples into those which belong to the category and those which do not. If, as in the case of countable and uncountable nouns, there are two contrasting categories, introduce the second and test if students understand that. Then ask students to divide words into the two categories. All of this has nothing to do with students producing language, or doing exercises. It is only ensuring that students understand, and can use, the terminology the teacher is going to use and which the students will themselves need.

After this initial introduction of the terms, the teacher should draw attention to the difficulties. In the case just mentioned this means pointing out that a noun is not *always* countable or uncountable. The same noun may have a countable meaning, and an uncountable meaning. Until students have grasped this, they do not have a clear understanding of the meaning of the terms.

No terminology should be taught for its own sake. It should provide teachers and students with a convenient shorthand. It can only do that if the terminology is taught and understood *before* students are expected to use it.

This problem is even more complex in referring to verb forms — English, for example, does not possess "a future tense". Several verb forms can be used to refer to Future Time:

I'm going to see him tomorrow.
I'm seeing him tomorrow.
I'll be seeing him tomorrow.

The term "the future tense", far from simplifying, will cause confusion because the term does not relate accurately to the structure of English.

Teachers should bear two rules in mind:

a. If a term is introduced, time needs to be taken to ensure that students really understand it. The terminology needs to be taught as part of the lesson.

b. A term should only be introduced if it is going to help the students. Terminology introduced to show off the teacher's knowledge, or simply because it sounds impressive, is dishonest and counter-productive.

5. Filling in a fill-in exercise is not enough

There are a number of objections to fill-in exercises, but, as long as they exist, it is better to do them well than badly. Such practices assume that the sentence which is given contains sufficient context to reveal the "correct" choice to be filled in. This means that elsewhere in the sentence there are clues to the correct answer — the part to be filled in in some way collocates with other words in the sentence. In such circumstances, it must be necessary for the student to say the whole sentence aloud, thereby increasing the chance of the item being memorised correctly.

It is incorrect for the teacher to give the number of the question, and the student simply to say the fill-in part; it is even worse for the teacher to read a sentence from the book and pause at the gap while the student says one or two words (the fill-in) before the teacher finishes the sentence.

Teachers may care to consider whether fill-in practices will be more effective if exploited three times — orally in class, as written homework, and finally checked again orally in class.

The students need the practice! The teacher should say the number; the students should say the *complete* example.

6. Students need to practise form as well as use

Language teaching has often had bandwagons. At one time the oral drill was thought to be extremely powerful — students became more accurate and fluent by repeating large numbers of examples which followed identical patterns. Contemporary methodology encourages us to be "communicative", and to ensure that all interchanges are "meaningful". As usual, the ideal lies somewhere between such extremes.

Language teaching based entirely on getting the forms correct becomes meaningless and boring, and has little to do with the real nature of language. At the same time it is difficult to be communicative if your hearer cannot understand what you say!

The teaching should maintain a balance between practices which concentrate on fluency, and those which concentrate on accuracy. On the whole, fluency practices concentrate on *why* a person is speaking (function) and accuracy practices on *how* the message is conveyed (structural form). A good language teaching programme involves both. Students have little difficulty in understanding that some verbs have irregular past tense forms, or how certain question forms are made in English. They also have little difficulty in understanding that the function *Getting information* involves asking questions. Neither of these bits of information, however, helps them actually to form questions accurately. Practising the forms — sometimes very uncommunicatively — is a legitimate part of a well-balanced teaching programme.

7. There is a place for oral and written practices

Traditional language teaching places great emphasis on writing long exercises to encourage familiarisation with particular structures. In reaction against that, however, much communicative teaching relies almost too exclusively on oral practice.

Oral practice is natural, and ensures that a wide range of structures co-occur, develops the ability to understand and respond quickly, and the ability to articulate — but it is not the whole of language teaching. Written practices, where the students have time to pause, think, and *consciously* construct, also have an important place. As usual in language learning, a policy of doing *both* activities, rather than one *or* the other, is best.

In general, it would usually be best for students first to do oral practice, then use written practice for reinforcement and, finally, further oral free practices.

It is worth emphasising that oral and written practices are both useful even if the students' main objective places the emphasis strongly on oral or written English. Clearly, the student who needs a high level in written skills requires more written practice than the general student, but in such a case oral practice provides a valuable alternative and supportive learning strategy. Similarly, for a student who requires a high level of oral skills, some written practice provides useful support which cannot be gained through a purely oral approach.

8. Use "gimmicks" to combat popular mistakes

Some mistakes are always "popular" — the third person-*s,* making questions, and, for each language group, certain interference mistakes, as students carry over too directly the patterns or vocabulary of their own language.

Such mistakes are rarely "important" from a communicative point of view, but may make the students sound odd, or may be mistakes which are heavily penalised in tests. In these cases it is usually better to combat the mistake by some kind of gimmick, rather than constantly explaining or taking a stern attitude.

Many teachers find it helpful to prepare a large card containing nothing but a very large letter **S**. This is kept flat on their desk and each time a student makes a third person-*s* mistake, the teacher, without speaking, simply raises the card; other teachers have a large **S** on the wall of their classroom and simply point to it.

A slightly more complicated "third person-*s*" card is illustrated opposite. This card emphasises that the -*s* is associated with *he, she* and *it.*

The second card illustrated, reminding students of irregular forms, is used when a student produces a sentence such as *He buyed it yesterday.* Teachers may like to prepare a similar card reminding students of the importance of **(do).**

If students find word order in questions difficult it can be effective to use a deliberately rather flamboyant gesture — the teacher holds out both arms and then crosses one over the other.

" Popular " mistakes can demotivate students — they " know " it is a mistake, but continue to make it. A light-hearted method of correction of such mistakes ensures that the mistake is drawn to the students' attention, without depressing students unnecessarily.

9. Use beehives with large classes

One of the most effective techniques for large classes is the beehive drill. Such practices work best in classes who are sitting in rows. A clear model is presented — either orally or on the blackboard:

> **How old are you?**
> **I'm . . .**

The model consists of a simple two-line dialogue. Then simultaneously, all the people sitting in a particular line, for example, next to the windows, ask the question to their neighbours; their neighbours answer and, without pausing, turn to their neighbours and ask the question; these students answer and, without pausing, pass the question on.

In this way six or seven pairs are involved at any one time and the whole class is involved in saying something (two sentences each) in a practice which lasts less than half a minute.

On other occasions the practice starts from the opposite side of the room or from the front or back of the classroom with the question being passed on to the student immediately behind or in front.

Such practices are only effective if the two-line dialogue is simple, and the model clear. The first time they are done they are often chaotic but as soon as the class has the idea of how such a practice works it is sufficient for the teacher to present the model and then say simply: *Beehive practice starting, here* (pointing).

The name of such practices is, of course, based on the fact that all the bees in the hive work at the same time. It is a model which is very appropriate for the language classroom!

10. Most language games are structure practices

It is characteristic of language games that the same formula is constantly repeated. That is precisely the same characteristic that is shown by structure practices!

A simple game like hangman is easily converted into a useful structure practice.

Each dash represents a letter; as letters are guessed, successful guesses are filled in, and for each unsuccessful guess part of the hanging scene is drawn. If the scene is completed before the word, the game is lost. The game is often used to help teach the alphabet. It can, however, be simply adapted to a very useful practice of *there*. Students use this formula:

Is there a (p) in it?   *There's a (p) here.*
No there isn't/Yes there is.   *There are two —,here and here.*

Instead of just calling out letters, the game has the extra rule that students must use the *Is there ... ?* formula in their questions.

A game such as *Who am I?* (one student 'is' a famous, person, alive or dead; the others try to guess who by asking questions which may be answered only *Yes* or *No*) provides practice of both questions with an auxiliary, and questions with **(do)**: *Are you American? Do you play the guitar?*

Teachers working with school classes often think that "games" can only be used for a few minutes at the end of a lesson, or occasionally on Friday afternoons. Almost all language games, with very little preparation from the teacher, can be turned into lively and effective structure practices. Needless to say, most students, particularly in schools, would rather play a game than do a grammar practice. Teachers should remember that if the students are enjoying what they're doing, and it has an underlying serious language teaching purpose, it is more likely to be effective than a more conventional practice.

11. Free situations are important

Most language lessons develop from controlled to free practice. Teachers like to be in control of their lessons and therefore like controlled practice. The lesson moves smoothly, can be timed carefully, and gives an impression of efficiency. Unfortunately, there is a big gap between controlled practice and natural language use. Natural language use involves not only knowledge of the language, but social skills, self-confidence, the ability to improvise, etc. Controlled practice is nothing more than a *first* step in the teaching sequence.

The free practice part of the lesson is, by definition, the part over which the teacher has least control. The students have more chance to make mistakes, to show that they have not learned, and to show that, even if they can do controlled practice, they have not yet developed the ability to use the language. Such practices — situations, dialogue building, information gap-based pair work, discussion, or writing about the student's own interests, are an essential part of the learning process. Such practices develop the whole range of skills which are required for effective natural language use. In doing them, teachers must encourage such skills, and not concentrate only on accurate structural knowledge. At the same time teachers should remember that these are still classroom practices. Neither the teacher nor the student should expect too much. They are an important step in the complex process which leads from structural accuracy to spontaneous fluency.

12. Grammar can be fun

Structure in the classroom involves finding, understanding, and using patterns. There is nothing very terrifying or inhibiting about that but, too often, students think of grammar as an unpopular and difficult part of their language lessons. Even more worryingly, that attitude is one they have usually caught from their teachers!

The last few tips have stressed that grammar practice can be both lively and amusing — providing the teacher brings a sense of fun to it and does such practice frequently, briskly and with a touch of humour.

Many students enjoy puzzles — crossword and word-search puzzle books have an enormous sale. The message is clear — many students enjoy looking for patterns, looking for similarities, sorting, pairing, and other typical puzzle activities. Most people feel a sense of some satisfaction at solving a puzzle but, at the same time, there is very little feeling of failure if you cannot do puzzles. Unfortunately, in the language classroom the exact opposite seems to apply — if you cannot do a grammar exercise there is a feeling of failure, but little satisfaction in doing well. Somehow or other, teachers (or "the system") fail to capitalise on the students' curiosity and enthusiasm. There may be many reasons for this, but two seem particularly important — teachers are too keen to evaluate — to give marks, so students simply fear failure. Secondly, too many grammar practices are not puzzle-like. They do not involve problem-solving, but all too frequently are nothing more than simple tests of pre-learned knowledge.

Puzzles and problems involve *not* knowing the answer, exploring, going up blind alleys, re-tracing your steps, often working with other people, and, eventually, finding a solution — perhaps *the* solution, or perhaps one of a set of alternative solutions. Problem-solving is challenging, amusing, frustrating, and frequently best done as a social activity. Those same words could very easily be applied to language learning. The teaching of structure can be made fun if, instead of the teacher *telling* students little bits of pre-digested "knowledge", students can be encouraged to explore and discover for themselves.

Practices which encourage the student to discover need not be original or imaginative. The emphasis is upon the teacher's attitude. At the lowest level, for example, students can be asked to go through the text and underline all examples of *is* and *are* which occur. Can students guess or work out the difference between them?

At a slightly higher level, the students can be asked to divide these examples into two groups:

Those with **(go)** used as a full verb.

Those with **(be) going to** used as an auxiliary.

1. He's going to the theatre.
2. Where are you going?
3. Are you really going to go?
4. What on earth are we going to do about it?
5. I think it's going to rain.
6. We hope we'll be going to Italy next summer.
7. Are you going to ask her?
8. Are you going on Saturday?

Instead of *explaining* to students that stress has an important part to play in conveying meaning, students can be asked to pair the remarks and responses in a practice such as the following. All they need to be told in advance is that there *is* a solution, and that there is only *one* solution — if they have done most of the examples and have a sentence left over which "will not fit", they must go back and do the whole practice again.

1. Does he know?   **a.** I've told him twice.
2. Why are you annoyed?   **b.** I have told him twice.
3. Shall we go?   **c.** That's David Bowie.
4. Why aren't you ready yet?   **d.** That is David Bowie.
5. Who's that?   **e.** I am ready.
6. Is David Bowie here?   **f.** Yes, I'm ready.

These examples illustrate the principle: the emphasis has moved from the teacher explaining to the student exploring. The latter is both more useful, and more fun. The more the teacher can change the emphasis of "grammar practices" in this way, the more students will enjoy and benefit from a part of the language lesson which all too often is unpopular.

13. Grammar is a receptive skill too

Usually when language teachers think of 'grammar', they think of doing activities which require students to produce correct sentences. Of course this is important, but it is not the whole story and, very importantly, it's not the **beginning** of the story. Very few language teachers nowadays think that you learn a grammar rule and are then able to apply it; the learning process is more complicated than that. The key word is 'process'— you hear some examples and partly understand, you hear an explanation which makes things a bit clearer, you forget a bit, partly understand some new examples and so on. Most grammar is not formally learned, but understanding builds up over a period. The student begins to see similarities and differences, where initially there was only confusion. This process of understanding is receptive not productive. With this in mind, and particularly with lower level classes, it is important to give students a chance to do some kind of receptive grammar work, helping them to listen or read more carefully but without the pressure of having to produce correct sentences immediately afterwards. If you do not understand the difference between *I live in Brighton* and *I am living in Brighton*, it is clear you will not be able to pro-duce that difference yourself. Sometimes, therefore, students should be exposed to some language — on tape or in written text — and then asked careful questions about what it means. The purpose is to focus their attention on the fact that grammar conveys meaning and, as well as understanding the words they also need to understand the grammar.

Most native speakers will 'feel'' an immediate difference between *What time will we arrive?* and *What time shall we arrive?* The first suggests the railway booking office, while the second suggests a party or other social arrangement. We hope this simple example will show that students need to be helped to develop this 'feel' or intuition. Grammar conveys meaning, but too often the teacher directs the students only to the meaning of words. Help your students to see the meaning of grammar as well.

14. Teach word grammar as well as sentence grammar

Teachers and students tend to divide language into grammar and vocabulary, but in some ways this is an artificial distinction. It is too easy to think that language consists of grammatical structures with slots in them where, once you have mastered the structures you can slot in the relevant words to say what you mean. Nothing could be further from the truth. In fact, thought is predominantly lexical, and when we speak we grammaticalise the words. If we make the artificial grammar/vocabulary distinction, and then think about meaning, it is easy to see that we must give primacy to the words. This suggests a useful teaching technique — think of the word *bus*. What other words do you associate with it? Before reading on, make a short list of perhaps the first five words that come into your mind.

Almost certainly, you will discover you have listed other nouns — *driver, bus stop, ticket* — but if you want to use the word *bus* in a sentence — in other words if you want to **talk about** a bus — these are not the words you will need. The words you will need then are the words which frequently co-occur with bus in the same sentence — their technical name is collocations. Typically, they will be adjectives and, most important of all, verbs. This means that when you learn the word *bus*, it would be useful to learn the verbs and adjectives with which it frequently collocates. It would be particularly useful if, instead of making a simple list of words in a vocabulary book, you recorded the words together which frequently occur together. This is best done in a simple shape like the one given below. Notice you can't combine any adjective with any verb with the noun but, by teaching the grammar of the word at the same time as the word you will make it much easier for the student to use the word in real natural sentences. Use a blank of the shape below to make your students vocabulary learning more closely related to the grammar they need, and consequently much more efficient.

catch	early	
get	first	
miss	next	bus
wait for	last	
take	number 13/24/etc	

Chapter 8

Techniques — Correction

Mark each of these statements before and after you read the chapter.
Mark each statement
        ✔ if you *agree*.
        X if you *disagree*.
        ? if you are *undecided*.

1. It is best to work so students make as few mistakes as possible.	
2. It is best to correct all the mistakes students make.	
3. It is useful to encourage students to correct each other.	
4. Mistakes are best corrected as soon as the student makes them.	
5. Too much correction is as bad as too little.	

Techniques — Correction

1. Mistakes are a natural part of the learning process

One of the major themes of this book is that language is a complex phenomenon, and language learning a correspondingly complex activity. Many
factors contribute towards the success or failure of the individual language
learner. One of the most important, however, is probably the confidence the
learner has in his ability to succeed in the task. We have already pointed out
in the introductory chapter that teachers frequently undermine this
confidence by emphasising the difficulties the student faces. Probably even
more important, however, in undermining the learners' confidence, is the
teacher's over-zealous correction of mistakes. At the simplest level
pronouncing a word in a totally new foreign language may involve putting
your mouth into a position it has never been in before. Inevitably it will
appear unnatural and few students will succeed. Most students learning a
foreign language, except the very young, bring with them the idea that the
new language will behave like their own mother tongue. If their own language
forms questions by inversion, it is easy to assume that this will be true in the
language they are learning. 'Interference' of this kind will mean that structural mistakes are inevitable.

At least within European languages, there are between any two languages
almost inevitably false friends — words which look or sound similar in the
two languages, but have very different meanings. Again, confusion is
inevitable.

The fact that confusions will arise does not mean they should remain
uncorrected, but it is important for the teacher to understand, and to feel
deeply, that mistakes are inevitable and a *natural* part of the learning process.
It is important for the teacher to transmit this attitude to students. The
student who is afraid of mistakes and remains silent will learn comparatively
little. The student who understands that learning involves making mistakes,
is more likely to make progress.

Teachers can help students to understand this by drawing parallels —
perhaps with children learning the students' native language, or with a quite
different area of learning such as the mechanical skill of serving at tennis. No-
one learning to play tennis expects *all* his first serves to go in, but the fact that
he occasionally overhits the ball does not mean that he gives up the game
and, indeed, even the Wimbledon champion overhits the ball occasionally.
Some of the skills of language learning are physical (motor) skills and require
a similar sort of practice.

It is essential that teachers transmit to students the idea that mistakes are an essential part of the learning process, and definitely *not* something to be feared.

The implications of the above remarks are particularly important for teachers working within a state school system which may require them to 'give marks' to their students. Teachers need to be very conscious of the fact that giving poor marks may itself contribute to the students' poor performance if the poor mark lowers their confidence in using the language. As far as possible, therefore, teachers who are required to give marks in this way should accompany their simple 'mark' by comments which encourage the student and avoid the de-motivating effect of the marks.

2. Give students the chance to correct themselves

Mistakes are of different kinds — some are only slips of the tongue, something which the student knows and will usually get right; some are the result of under-learning, others the result of over-learning; some are the result of students completely mis-understanding either some aspect of the language, or the instructions as to what is required of them for a particular practice. In every case if the teacher jumps in immediately with a correction, an opportunity for real understanding is lost.

It is usually sufficient if the student makes a mistake and the teacher decides it is worth correcting immediately to stop the student either by a facial expression or a hand gesture such as shaking a finger. Before doing anything else the teacher should pause and wait. If the student can correct him- or herself nothing more needs to be said. The main principle of correction is that self-correction is best.

3. Involve the class

If the student is not able to provide self-correction the teacher should invite other students in the class to comment before providing the correct language. There are a number of important reasons for this — it helps to keep all the class involved while an individual is answering a question; by involving students in correcting each other it makes clear that language learning for them is a corporate activity and, however competitive their examinations may be, their actual language lessons do not need to be competitive in that way. Finally, and significantly, it reduces the element of teacher domination which is inevitable with over-zealous teacher correction.

4. Isolate the problem

If it becomes necessary for the teacher to provide a correction it is essential to do so in the most helpful manner possible. If a student has made a small mistake in a whole sentence — this means *most* of what the student said was correct. Isolating the mistake both helps to correct, and avoids the de-motivating effect of suggesting that all of what the student said was unsatisfactory.

Even after the individual student and class have failed to provide self-correction, it is still not necessary for the teacher to give the correction. The teacher can repeat the incorrect utterance and, by pausing immediately before or after the mistake, highlight it in the hope that this will be sufficient help to encourage a student to produce the correct answer. More explicitly, the teacher may name the mistake precisely: *Peter and Jill is in the garden — Not 'is'*. . . Only as a last resort does the teacher give the correct answer.

In the case of pronunciation mistakes it must be emphasised that isolating the mistake involves not only isolating the particular word which was said wrongly, but the particular sound. While every attempt should be made to encourage students to correct themselves, the process is never one of trying to trick students. The teacher's constant strategy should be to direct the students' attention towards the mistake while, at the same time, not simply jumping in with a correction.

5. The student must use the correct language

If the student corrects himself he inevitably does repeat the correct form. If some other member of the class provides the correct answer, the teacher must invite the student who made the mistake to say the complete correct form — *complete* to help fix collocational features in the student's memory, and the *correct* repetition to ensure that the *last* thing the student has said is the correct version and it is this which is likely to stay in the student's memory.

If the teacher corrects, it is essential that the student repeats the full correct form. Sometimes one hears the following:

S   I buyed it in London.
T   No, not buyed, bought.
S   Yes.
T   . . . can you do the next question please?

Such a correction is useless. The only person who has said the correct form is the teacher. There is no evidence that the student even understands the correction — most students realise that saying *Yes* is more likely to please the teacher than saying *No!*

The transcription of a full correction of even a simple mistake can appear laborious but note that it involves everyone, and, done fairly quickly, is more interesting and effective than any long explanation from the teacher.

T   Where did he buy it?
S   He buyed it from London.
T   *(indicates mistake by facial expression or gesture).*
S   He buyed it from London.
T   Can anybody help?
S2   In London.
T   That's right — anything else?
C   *Silence.*
T   Not **buyed** — anybody?
S2   Boughted.
T   *(smiles)* No — nearly . . . anybody?
S3   Bought.
T   That's right. Everbody . . .**bought.**
C   Bought.
T   Again.
C   Bought

T	So where did he buy it?
S1	He bought it from London.
T	*(smiles and shakes head)* No — not **from,** S2?
S2	In.
T	*(nods, and looks at S1).*
S1	He bought it in London.
T	Good, everybody.
C	He bought it in London.
T	*(looks at S1 again)*
S1	He bought it in London.

This process may take time, but it must be emphasised that the object of classroom activity is language *learning,* not language teaching. It is the students whose performance is to be improved and the process described above involves the students, helps them to increase their confidence, and encourages *them* to use the correct form. The teacher who jumps in and gives a correct answer 'to keep the lesson moving' has lost sight of the basic objective of what teachers are doing. (see also Re-formulation, page 95)

6. There are many kinds of mistakes

Teachers often worry about *when* to correct but an equally, if not more, important question is *what* to correct. Traditionally, language teachers have concentrated on certain types of mistake — poor pronunciation, wrong choice of vocabulary, and, most importantly of all, structural errors. While these are important, there are other kinds of mistake which may, on occasion, be more important.

The kinds of mistake listed above are usually 'obvious', and, as such, rarely destroy communication. With the increasing emphasis on communicative language teaching, however, certain other mistakes which are often very important to the communication, need to be considered. Here are some of the most important:

Stress
It is frequently more difficult to listen to and understand someone whose stress patterns are non-standard than somebody who produces individual sounds in a non-standard way.

Intonation
Intonation is important in English, particularly to express emotion and attitude, both of which are frequently very important in oral communication. The student who is more advanced — has good vocabulary, structure, and pronunciation — but who uses flat, uninteresting intonation will frequently be misunderstood — not in terms of the factual content of the message, but, more importantly, in terms of attitude.

Register and appropriacy
Certain language is appropriate only to certain situations, or for use with certain people. Once again, more advanced students can give the wrong impression of their attitude to other people or to a topic by the choice of grammatically correct but inappropriate language. Such students will need to be 'corrected' in the sense that they will need to be given *alternative* more appropriate ways of expressing themselves.

Omissions

With free communicative practice, pair work, or situations, frequently the most important 'mistakes' are things which students do *not* say. The student whose English is otherwise good who uses *I want one of those* to ask for something in a shopping situation will give an unfortunate impression. The student needs to be corrected by being asked to say something different, and above all by being reminded that the omission of *please* is important.

The distinction between fluency and accuracy needs constantly to be borne in mind. But particularly for students who are good intermediate or advanced, the teacher needs to have a much wider concept of mistakes than simply correcting pronunciation, vocabulary or structural error.

7. Correcting register and appropriacy needs tact

Few students will be upset if the teacher corrects their use of vocabulary or structure. The same is not always true when the teacher corrects register or appropriacy. A smile and pleasant manner help, but even so, some students react strongly if the teacher says *No, you can't say that. You could say that to somebody you knew very well but to somebody you don't know very well it sounds rather aggressive. It seems a bit rude.*

As adults few of us are used to having our behaviour criticised. We are not used to being told we are 'rude'. The teacher above did *not* say the student was rude, but that if the student used a particular language item in certain circumstances it might *seem* rude. Although students may understand this intellectually, it can still upset them. The temptation is then for the teacher to stop making corrections of this kind. If a teacher does not correct mistakes of this kind in the classroom, students will continue to make them outside the classroom, sometimes in situations where people will not allow for the fact that the speaker is not a native speaker.

It helps if a teacher explains to students that such corrections are *language* mistakes and the teacher is not making any sort of personal criticism.

8. Correct promptly for accuracy, afterwards for fluency

In the introductory chapter we emphasised the difference between accuracy and fluency practices. The former emphasise language learning — the conscious study and production of 'correct' forms; the latter emphasise a more unconscious spontaneous language use. These descriptions — conscious versus unconscious — automatically suggest that it will be appropriate to correct immediately during accuracy practices, but to avoid disturbing the spontaneity of fluency practices.

In practices which concentrate on accuracy it is usually best for the teacher to indicate a mistake immediately — usually by facial expression or gesture.

Most teachers feel confident about picking up structural or pronunciation errors and are frequently too keen to correct these. In the case of fluency practices — often called situations, communicative practices, free practices, etc — teachers should keep a small pad of paper beside them and make a note of one or two important mistakes. They may be 'important' for different reasons:

a. They are common to several members of the class.

b. They are likely to create genuine misunderstanding if not corrected.

c. They show a gap in the students' knowledge — i.e. they are not positive mistakes which the students make, but things which it is clear they cannot say because they do not have the appropriate word or phrase and the lack of this item seriously impedes the communicative effectiveness of what they are trying to say.

In such practices it is usually wise to pick on one or two 'important' mistakes of these kinds and to discuss them *after* the practice. In some cases it may be appropriate to ask the students to repeat the practice (in the case of communicative pair work, or other forms of situational practice).

If teachers keep in mind the distinction between activities which are aimed at accuracy and those which are aimed at fluency and boosting students' confidence, the 'problem' of when and what to correct becomes common sense.

9. Don't over-correct

In the first tip of this section it was emphasised that mistakes are a natural part of the learning process. Over-emphasis on correction by the teacher can have a de-motivating effect. The implication is clear — it is the teacher's job to select those mistakes which are worth correcting within the context in which they are produced.

On the whole, if an accuracy practice is at the right level for the students it will be possible to correct most, if not all, of the mistakes. If they are making too many mistakes it suggests that the material has not been adequately prepared and presented by the teacher, and rather than continuing with the practice, it may be wiser to break off and re-present the material.

In the case of fluency practices teachers must expect that students will make a large number of errors of all types. It would be disastrous to make a list of all of these and then go through them systematically after the practice. In the previous section we discussed some criteria for 'important' mistakes. Using those — and perhaps other criteria which are important in your particular situation — two or three mistakes should be selected and the student's attention concentrated upon those. In this way students realise that they are monitored by the teacher during free practice; they see that free practice in which they make mistakes does help the teacher to help them; but a depressing barrage of small corrections is avoided.

10. Re-formulation is often better than correction

In this technique, the teacher responds naturally to what is said, and in passing provides the correct language but, in direct contrast to the earlier suggestion (5 above), deliberately **avoids** getting the student to repeat in an artificial, language-learning way.
Here is an example:

S   My mummy buyed it for me.
T   Oh, that's nice, your Mummy bought it for you, did she.
S   Yes.
T   Where did she buy it?
S   She buyed it in town.
T   Oh she bought it in town for you. Well it's very nice.

Readers may be confused in that the re-formulation technique seems almost to be the opposite of that discussed earlier, and this is indeed the case. As time goes by, more and more people believe that you are **acquire** grammar — build up an unconscious and developing understanding of how to use it — largely on the basis of your language input — what you hear and read. You take in more of the input if you are relaxed. If you believe this (as we do) you will almost always prefer re-formulation to formal correction.

Inexperienced teachers need to practise re-formulation. The closer your response is to a natural human response, while still being at the student's linguistic level, the more effective it is likely to be.

11. Use a code to correct written work

Correction is more likely to be effective, and less intimidating if you devise a simple code which you can write in the margin for drawing the student's attention to surface errors — **sp** for a spelling mistake; **gr** for a grammar mistake etc. Obviously, you will often not want to mark every mistake, but to simply use your code to highlight important mistakes. When students get their work back they should then be asked to see if they can identify the mistakes themselves, with the help of your code.

One of the ways that you can help students improve their written work most effectively, is to take a short part of what they have written, and re-write it yourself, **as you would have written it**, without regard to what they have actually written linguistically, taking only the content of what they say. Just going back over their mistakes is likely to be less effective than looking at a simple short piece of language well constructed which they can compare with their own.

12. Use class discussion as a method of correcting written work

As an alternative to marking mistakes in exercises or essays, teachers may prefer this technique. The teacher types out say a dozen sentences, six of which are correct and contain language which is taken from the exercise or essays, and six of which contain 'typical' mistakes, made by a number of students in their work. The correct and incorrect sentences should be mixed together. The sheets are copied, and then given to small groups of students — pairs or groups of 3/4 students. The students' task is to identify the correct sentences, and to correct the mistakes in ones which contain mistakes.

It will be quickly appreciated that this activity is more involving, and more demanding, than simply looking through your own work covered in red ink.

As with so many of the techniques in this chapter, the purpose is to contribute to the students' long-term language learning, rather than to concentrate on 'quick fix' correcting. Language learning is more important than language teaching — more important than either is the language learner — all techniques of correction should be used with that thought constantly in mind.

Chapter 9

Techniques — Vocabulary

Mark each of these statements before and after you read the chapter.
Mark each statement
> ✓ if you *agree.*
> X if you *disagree.*
> ? if you are *undecided.*

1. Students need to know the difference between active and passive vocabulary.	
2. Words are best taught in groups of similar meaning.	
3. The best way to explain is to translate.	
4. English-English explanations are best.	
5. An English-English dictionary is an important aid for students.	

Techniques — "Vocabulary"

1. A "vocabulary" item can be more than one word

Most teachers are familiar with the fact that their students believe, or at least seem to believe, that direct word-for-word translations are possible. There is a temptation to think that a foreign language is nothing more than using new words for old things. In fact, of course, it is much more complicated than that.

In relatively formal circumstances two speakers of (British) English meeting for the first time will both say *How do you do. How do you do* is a complete phrase with a single meaning — linguists would call it a lexical item (i.e. a phrase the meaning of which may be looked up in the lexicon). The meaning of this group of words cannot be deduced from the meaning of the individual words used in the phrase — *how,* for example, at first suggests that the phrase will be a question (the phrase is sometimes printed in textbooks with a question mark at the end of it!) but since both speakers use the *same* phrase, it is quite clear that neither is a question, each is a greeting. Such groups of words are common and, rather than keeping a list of "words" in a "vocabulary book", students need to be encouraged to keep lists of words and *phrases* (i.e. lexical items) with, in some cases, direct equivalents in their own language but in other cases simply a description of how the phrase is used — in the case above a definition such as "a greeting used by both speakers when meeting for the first time in fairly formal circumstances".

Such phrases are of great importance in both the written and spoken language and students should be encouraged to see them as whole items. Further examples are phrases such as:

I'm afraid not	Cheer up!
I'd rather you didn't, if you don't mind	put up with
If you like	look out for (someone)

Some phrases lie on the boundary between phrases which may be seen as part of the structure of the language, and phrases which can be learned as single units. An example of such a phrase would be: *as soon as possible.*

In many cases students can be helped to achieve greater fluency by learning certain phrases as complete items at a relatively early stage in their learning programme, while perhaps only seeing or understanding their structure at a later stage.

The important thing is to develop in the students an understanding that languages do not consist of "words" with equivalents from one language to the other.

2. Do not discuss the structure of lexical items

Some years ago teaching was almost entirely based on structural progression. Students learned *Do you want ...?* relatively early in their course, because it was an example of a question made in the present simple, which comes early in most structural courses. It was only relatively late in their course that they learned *Would you like ...?* because this was "a conditional" which, in turn, came relatively late in structurally orientated courses.

One of the positive results of the notional/functional approach to language teaching has been to point out that students frequently need certain language items for practical communication relatively early in their course even if these items may seem structurally quite complex. It is now quite common for phrases such as *would you like* to appear in Book 1 under a functional heading. There is no difficulty about this providing teachers explain the phrase by explaining its *function* — "We use this when we want to offer somebody something — *would you like a cup of tea*? or when we want to invite them to do something — *would you like to go to the cinema this evening*?" Such an explanation is sufficient, and teachers must resist the temptation to draw attention to the *structural* features of the phrase which is being taught *as a lexical item* at that stage of the course.

In the case of *How do you do* it can only confuse students to point out that it *appears* to have the structure of a question — *all* the student needs to know is the meaning (i.e. the use) of the lexical item. In a similar way it is not necessary when introducing *Would you like* in Book 1, to make a remark such as *You'll learn about the structure of this later.* As far as the students are concerned, they know what they need to know if they know how to use the particular phrase. Teachers who themselves learned foreign languages in a very strongly structuralist tradition must avoid confusing their students by using structuralist explanations for functional materials.

3. There is a difference between active and passive vocabulary

Well-educated native speakers "know" many thousands of words in the sense that when they hear or read them they cause no difficulty in understanding. At the same time the same people probably use only about 2,000 words in normal daily conversation. Somewhat surprisingly, native speaker command of as small a vocabulary as 2,000 words means that you can function quite happily within an English speaking community — providing the command is comprehensive, and the 2,000 items are the **right** 2,000!

"Learning" more and more vocabulary items does not necessarily increase a person's fluency. By definition, the extra items are less and less useful. Despite this obvious fact, teachers, and even more so students, feel that increasing their vocabulary will increase their fluency — either in speech or in writing. This is very far from the truth.

"Knowing" a vocabulary item is not a simple process — it means much more than simply memorising the word. From a receptive (passive) point of view, it means recognising its meaning when it occurs in context — a relatively simple process. For students to add the word to their active vocabularies they need to know the contexts in which it can occur, the possible and impossible collocations of the word (words it can, or cannot, co-occur with) as well as more details of the connotational meaning of the word.

In a very simple sense *little* and *small* "mean the same thing" — most students of English have no difficulty understanding the sentence *Which would you like — the big one or the small/little one?* Even such "simple" words, however, present difficulties for active use — it is possible to say *What a pretty little dress,* but not **What a pretty small dress.*

In the spoken language there is a spectrum from "standard" English, through colloquial and idiomatic use down to slang. Students who are going to use their language with native speakers may well need to *understand* certain idiomatic and colloquial language, possibly even a certain amount of slang, but as a general rule they will sound extremely odd if they incorporate slang into their own active vocabularies.

The message for the teacher is that in dealing with "new words", it is helpful to guide students towards those words which it will help them to add to their active vocabularies, and to distinguish those for students from the much larger number of passive items. At the beginning of most conventional language courses, *all* the words which are taught are intended to be acquired for active use; later, at intermediate and advanced levels, *most* of the words students meet will only be needed for passive use. This change in the nature of the vocabulary they are learning is rarely made clear to students.

In more modern courses, particularly those which emphasise listening skills based on authentic material even early in courses, a distinction between active and passive language must be made at a much earlier stage. It is an important part of the listening process that students learn to understand items which they do *not* need to add to their active vocabularies.

4. Explain difference of meaning, not meaning

Understanding or explaining "what something means" is more complicated than teachers or students sometimes recognise. There is a temptation, for example, for teachers to "explain" a word by a direct translation. It is exceptionally rare for a word in one language to have a direct equivalent in another. Much translation-based teaching ignores this, and encourages the idea of simple equivalents.

Language is a system and each word has its meaning defined in relation to other words. This insight leads to an easier, more effective and theoretically sounder way of explaining. It is always more helpful to explain *difference of meaning* rather than meaning itself. If the reader is in any doubt then try to explain the meaning of *bush*. It is easy if done visually **and** *contrastively*:

tree   bush

This is of practical importance not only in dealing with vocabulary, but also in discussing the major structural features of the language. The textbook may present the present simple in unit 6 and the present continuous in unit 7, but the student has in no sense mastered either until he also understands the *difference* between them.

The principle is that *contrastive* explanation is easier, more efficient, and most importantly of all, reflects the real nature of language.

5. Words are often best taught in groups

An individual word in a language frequently acquires a meaning because of the relationship between it and other words. Awareness of certain kinds of relationship makes explaining vocabulary easier for the teacher, and learning it simpler for the student. Here are some important relationships:

a. Synonyms. These are by no means as frequent as people think. Though words may have similar denotative meaning (they represent the same concept) their connotational meanings often differ. Sometimes, however, it is possible for the teacher simply to say *'Enormous' means the same as 'very large'.*

b. Antonyms. These are often thought of as "opposites" such as *hot/cold.* It is important for teachers to remember that *not hot,* does not always mean *cold;* sometimes it is a question of degree. In these cases students usually start by learning the extremes and later learn intermediate words: *hot — warm — cool — cold.*

c. Complements. Here two words exist and one automatically excludes the other — *single/married.* In this case it is possible to explain by saying *'Single' means 'not married'.*
This idea may be extended to groups of incompatible words — each is defined by being "not the others": *morning — afternoon — evening — night.* Obviously it is best to teach such words in groups, as the meaning of one depends directly on the meaning of the others.

d. Converses. Each of a pair of words implies the other: *parent/child, employer/employee.* Again, such words are best explained together.

e. Hyponyms. *Car, van, bus, lorry* are hyponyms of *vehicle.* Often, such words are difficult to handle without translating. It is not much help to be told *a carnation is a kind of flower.* If you want to know the meaning of the word you want to know *what* kind of flower. In such cases translation is often necessary.

These theoretical ideas may often be usefully extended by the idea of an *Area of Vocabulary.* If, for example, students are to do some work on traffic it makes sense to pre-teach the vocabulary and lexis associated with the topic. Because many words are defined by their relationship to other words, it is easier to teach vocabulary in 'areas' than through lists of isolated items.

6. Vary the way you explain

It is probably true that the most difficult and most ineffective means of explaining vocabulary are the most widely used — these are translation, giving a synonym, and providing a verbal explanation. There are occasions when each is appropriate, but more occasions when there are more interesting, more effective, and more memorable ways of explaining new vocabulary, and helping to fix it in students' minds.

a. Demonstrate

There is something ridiculous about providing a translation or explanation of words such as *stagger, chuckle*. If the teacher does give a verbal explanation, it should at least be accompanied by a physical demonstration. The demonstration both helps to make the meaning clearer, and helps to fix the word in the students' minds.

It is not unusual for students to be able to tell you where they learned a new word, what the weather was like on the day, etc. The more the student can be involved as a person in what is going on in the language classroom, the more likely the new language is to be retained effectively in the memory. If every word is "explained" in the same way — either by translation or verbal explanation — they merge into a sea of language in which it is difficult to distinguish individual items. Demonstration highlights a particular word and helps associate it in the students' minds with both visual and aural memories.

b. Use the real thing

Teachers become so pre-occupied with teaching that sometimes they explain, or even draw on the blackboard things which are immediately available in the room. Sometimes the explanation is no more complicated than pointing!

c. Draw or sketch

Teachers do not need to be artists to make simple sketches which illustrate meaning — particularly if they bear in mind the advice given above about teaching contrast rather than meaning itself. The meaning of *bush* was explained by two very simple sketches.

d. Use the blackboard to show scales or grades

Words like *cool, orange* (colour), or *probably* may be explained by presenting them with groups of related words:

hot	*red*	*certainly / definitely*
warm	*orange*	*probably / possibly*
cool	*yellow*	
cold		

e. Antonyms

Teachers, particularly native teachers, trained within the British "O-level English" tradition instinctively look for a synonym when trying to explain a word. There are two problems — firstly there are very few exact synonyms within the language and, as mentioned above, it is easy to give the wrong impression by, for example, equating *little* and *small*. Secondly, in most cases it is extremely difficult to find a synonym which is simple enough to help the student — there is little point in simply providing another new word to explain the one the student does not understand!

It is usually much easier to offer explanations of the kind *Rude means not polite.*

It is worth mentioning that the explanations given here are not exact definitions of the word — the level of the explanation must be suitable to the students' level of English at the time so that dictionary-like accuracy can often be counter-productive.

f. Synonyms
Sometimes it is helpful particularly with a relatively unimportant word of passive vocabulary to provide a quick synonym explanation. It is still helpful if teachers remember to say *It is similar in meaning to . . .* , rather than *It means the same as . . .* , The former phrase helps to build up in the student's mind the idea that language consists of choice, that words do not mean the same as each other; the second undermines this important attitude.

g. The dictionary
Too often teachers forget that it is the students who are learning and, in general, the more the students are involved in the process the more successful that is likely to be. Texts should not contain very large numbers of new words (see page 106) so there should not be a great number of new words at any one time. One technique for explaining these which teachers too frequently overlook is asking the class whether anybody knows the word — individual students do learn things outside the classroom — and, if not, asking one or more students to look the word up in a dictionary (at lower levels a bi-lingual dictionary; at higher levels a mono-lingual dictionary). In this way the process of "learning a new word" also provides practice in important learning skills — dictionary using — and, for those using a good mono-lingual dictionary — ensures that they do have other examples for words used in context, a note on its stress, etc.

h. Verbal explanations
Some language items are best explained by being used in a *variety* of contexts, with the teacher commenting on the use. It is important with such explanations to use more than one context to avoid any incidental features of that particular context.

   This kind of explanation is particularly useful in dealing with the lexical items common within functional teaching. Most "functional phrases" are best explained by two or three examples and a description of the function performed. It is not usually necessary to add further explanation.

i. Translation
Although some teachers over-use this technique, it is equally true that others under-use it. To some it is seen as boring and traditional. For some words, however, the only sensible way to explain is by translation — this is often the case with certain types of technical words — *measles* — and for words which are "a kind of . . . " e.g. *oak.*

There is a rich variety of ways of "explaining new words". A number of factors need to be borne in mind:

a. Is the word for active or passive use by the students?

b. Is your intention to explain an unexpected difficulty without disturbing the main flow of the lesson, or is the vocabulary studied the main point of the particular classroom activity?

Teachers need to be aware of a variety of ways of explaining, and constantly to ask themselves **why** a particular word is being explained at all.

7. Words can link grammatically as well as thematically

We have already discussed teaching words in groups, but to most teachers and students this will mean thematic linking — all the words you associate with football, all the things you can find in the kitchen, the parts of a car and so on. Of course this is better than just random vocabulary, but as we pointed out earlier (page 88) it is particularly helpful to teach words which co-occur at the same time. It is worth re-emphasising the fact that words can link grammatically — write down five adjectives which you think frequently co-occur with *book*. Write five verbs too. What prepositions regularly follow the word *book?*

If you are a book publisher you will think of technical, job-related verbs such as *launch, edit, reprint,* but all of us would recognise the usefulness of a sentence such as *I've just finished an absolutely fascinating book about the Aztecs.* But it will be astonishingly difficult to produce such a sentence if your language learning has taught you some vocabulary — in this case the word *book* — and some grammar — in this case the present perfect. The ability to use the language depends on the ability to **bring grammar and vocabulary together.** So it must make sense sometimes to teach words which are **grammatically** linked rather than concentrating on thematic linking. As we saw earlier, this involved short lists — perhaps five items — giving adjectives and verbs which regularly co-occur with a noun. Sometimes too other words naturally suggest themselves — in this case *a book about ... by ...* .

Too often, vocabulary learning seems to the students to be an un-ending, totally disorganised process of learning thousands of different items. By thinking of grammatical links, vocabulary can, at least to a limited extent, be systematised.

8. Record words together which occur together

This is a direct extension of the above point, and a reminder of the box on page 88. Here is another example:

finish	*marvellous*		*on*	*the War.*
borrow	*fascinating*		*about*	*Mozart*
buy	*boring*	*book*		
study	*super*			*Jeffery Archer.*
struggle through	*heavy*		*by*	*Jane Austen.*

Chapter 10

Techniques — Texts

Mark each of these statements before and after you read the chapter.
Mark each statement

           ✔ if you *agree.*
           X if you *disagree.*
           ? if you are *undecided.*

1. Texts are for presenting new language to students.	
2. It is better for a text to be too easy than too difficult.	
3. It is useful to ask some questions about a text *before* reading it.	
4. Unseen reading aloud helps students' pronunciation.	
5. "I see no use for *silent* reading in class."	
6. Pronunciation practice *before* comprehension questions!	
7. Comprehension questions should use the language of the text.	
8. Good comprehension questions often expect the answer '*No*'	
9. Mix comprehension and conversation questions about students themselves!	
10. Textbook texts don't usually help students to *read* better.	

Techniques — Texts

1. Different texts have different uses

Different texts are suitable for different activities. For many teachers "the text" is the presentation part of the lesson. It introduces new language, and provides the basis for later language work and discussion. Teachers used to this idea of a text usually expect the text to be specially written, the language to be carefully graded, and certain new language features to be heavily recycled. Such an approach to text is, however, very narrow. Texts are of many different kinds — menus, instructions, signs, information, stories, advertisements, hand-written notes, letters, telexes, reports. The list is almost endless. Each of these types of text is different from the others in purpose, and also different in structure and language. If students are really going to use their English outside the classroom they will need to be able to handle these different types of texts, not only those specially prepared for language teaching textbooks.

In a similar way the skills that are required to handle different types of texts are themselves very varied. Traditional language teaching has seen intensive study of specifically prepared texts. Modern theories suggest a wide range of activities which are appropriate to different kinds of text.

Sometimes, for example, we look at texts only to check particular items of information (What time does the theatre start? How long do I need to cook the mixture for?)

Sometimes we start but do not finish texts — often in newspapers we find we skim quickly through picking out individual words, and decide that the topic is not of interest to us.

Sometimes, we are not interested in the detail of an article but only in its conclusion, and it is sufficient to read the last paragraph where the conclusions are summarised.

The teacher who uses texts in class only to present the language for intensive study is not teaching students to use the language. Effective language teaching means using different techniques to practise different skills for different types of text. Teachers who are interested in developing their students' reading skills should refer to a more extensive discussion of this such as *Teaching Reading Skills, Christine Nuttall, Heinemann.*

2. Too many new words make a text impossible

Most language teachers have, as students, had the experience of using a dictionary with a text containing a high density of new items and, after checking all the new words, still having little or no idea of the meaning of the text as a whole! Although it may be a good idea to leave students to guess the meaning of a *few* words from context, in order to do this they have first to be able to understand the *majority* of the text.

If there are more than about 6 new words per 100 "running words" (i.e. all the words of the text) it is too difficult. Difficulty does not increase with the number of new words as in figure 1, but much more rapidly, as in figure 2.

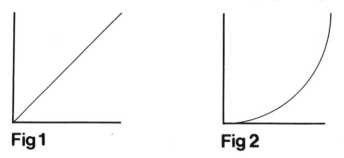

Fig 1   **Fig 2**

No matter how much preparation is done on a passage containing too many new items, it will not help significantly. Too much new material simply cannot be mastered at one time.

3. Nothing is 'interesting' if you can't do it

Teachers are often keen, particularly when looking for texts for their students, to find something 'interesting'. Although the aim is a good one, there is a serious difficulty attached to it. The teacher who finds an article in a newspaper or magazine is frequently tempted to use it with a class. It is important to remember before you do this that your vocabulary is probably at least twice that of even the best foreign learners below university level.

The criterion for choosing a text must be 'will *these students* find this interesting?' The answer to that question cannot possibly be *'Yes'* unless those students can understand it without great difficulty.

Every teacher has on some occasion taken in a piece of supplementary material which he thought would suit the class only to find that it is, in fact, far too difficult for them. In those circumstances there is only one thing to do — abandon that piece of material with that class, forget your lesson plan, and do something else.

Nothing is more depressing than struggling word-by-word at snail's pace through a piece of material so that you can do something with it or talk about it only to find that understanding the material has taken so long that the interesting follow-up activity lasts only a moment or two or disappears altogether.

4. Use pre-activities to focus students' attention

All language use in real life occurs in situations which allow the language user to rely heavily on anticipation and context. It is correspondingly artificially difficult to ask students to read an unseen text with no preparation. Good text preparation involves:

a. Introduction

The teacher gives a *brief* (two or three sentences) introduction to the *content* of the text. If the "text" is in dialogue form, the teacher mentions the situation in which the dialogue takes place, the number of speakers, and if necessary, something about their relationship (friends, strangers, etc). If the text is a chapter of a continuous story, ask the class or individual students to re-cap the story so far.

If the text is a one-off with a headline, ask the students what they *think* it is going to be about and (briefly) if they know anything about the topic. Many well-designed modern textbooks use photographs or other illustrations which help to indicate the general content of the text. Teachers should, if necessary, specifically draw attention to these and help students to bring to mind vocabulary and ideas which will occur in the text.

b. Pre-questions

Pre-questions are comprehension questions asked *before* the students read the text. They help students understand the text by focusing attention on key words and ideas.

Two or three pre-questions are enough. These questions should follow the main story-line or line of argument in the text and be in the correct sequence. They are intended to indicate the basic structure of the text, and help students' anticipation. In this way they make the reading of the text more natural.

c. Vocabulary

Teachers sometimes pre-teach certain new words which occur in the text. This can be helpful, particularly if one or two words which are known to be new occur frequently in the text.

More generally useful, however, is to invite students to anticipate vocabulary themselves. This may be done by using word-ladders, or word-roses. For these a word which is central to the content of the text is written at the top of the ladder, or in the centre of the rose like this:

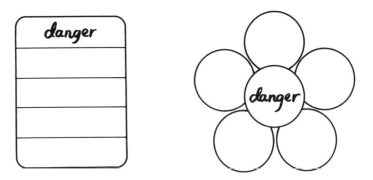

Students then fill in the other "steps" of the ladder, or "petals" of the rose. In the case of the ladder, each word they fill in should be connected to the previous step; in the case of the rose each word must be connected to the central word. At lower levels most students will provide the same group of words but at intermediate levels and upwards students may provide very different sequences or groups.

After they have completed the ladder or rose, various students are asked what words they have filled in. If some students do not know words used by others they are encouraged to ask each other about the unknown words; it can also be amusing to let students ask each other to explain *how* they constructed the sequence of the word-ladder.

Of course many of the words introduced in this way will not occur in the text but, if the first word has been well chosen, students will remind themselves of several important vocabulary items before reading the text. This kind of vocabulary focus, in which the language user brings to mind words he thinks will be useful, is typical of natural language use. Ladders and roses provide an amusing way of previewing vocabulary, and provide an excellent part of the general preparation for text study.

5. Distinguish between intensive and extensive reading

Intensive reading means students are expected to understand everything they read and to be able to answer detailed vocabulary and comprehension questions.

Extensive reading means students have a general understanding of the text *without* necessarily understanding every word. Intensive reading helps to improve extensive reading, but the latter also needs to be practised in its own right, principally to give students confidence in dealing with authentic materials.

It is sometimes appropriate to introduce material specifically for extensive reading practice. More common, however, is to use *part* of a longer text for extensive practice, and a different part for intensive practice. Too often teachers plough through the text in a uniform fashion, dealing with all the material intensively, thereby ensuring it takes too long, interest is lost, and an important language skill which needs to be practised is ignored.

Even if a text is to be dealt with largely intensively, it helps to encourage students to get a general understanding first by using pre-questions. In the early stages of students' learning programmes it is helpful to introduce texts containing some unknown language, but where students will know enough to understand the gist. Having taken such a text into class, however, it is then essential that the teacher is *not* tempted to explain all the words, or to ask too many questions. All that needs to be done is to encourage students to pick out particular information and, equally important, to encourage students *not* to worry at ignoring other, perhaps quite large, sections of the text which are not relevant to the task they have been given.

Teachers used to a traditional, structural, approach expect the texts of their textbooks to be carefully structurally graded. The implicit assumption is that *all* the material in the textbook will be dealt with intensively. It is particularly important for these teachers to realize that when authentic material is presented at an early stage in modern textbooks, its objectives are different and, if they approach such material intensively, they will de-motivate their students, and create problems for their students and themselves. On the other hand, if they approach such material extensively they will see that it can have a very positive effect on their students, who realize that, even with the little English at their disposal, they can actually *use* "real" English language materials.

6. Do not ask students to read aloud unseen

Reading aloud is a very difficult skill. Unseen texts probably contain new vocabulary items which students will not know how to pronounce; dialogues may require particular intonation patterns unfamiliar to students. Unprepared reading will be hesitant, unnatural and difficult for other students to follow.

Asking a student to read aloud unseen also means that he may concentrate so hard on pronouncing the words that he will be unable to concentrate adequately on their meaning too. He may read correctly but afterwards will not be able to tell you what he has read!

The first reading is best done by the teacher or on tape. Alternatively the class may prepare silently, with the teacher helping individuals with difficulties. Prepared reading will always be more effective than unseen and preparation time is certainly not wasted.

7. Vary the method of reading

There are many more ways of "reading" a text than asking a student *You start . . . Can you carry on please.*

The simplest method of reading, frequently forgotten by language teachers, is *silent* reading. It is the method we normally use with our native language, and on the whole the quickest and most efficient. It is the only method which is appropriate for *extensive* reading.

It can, however, also be appropriate for *part* of the intensive reading of a text — in this case, usually with a relatively simple part of the text where silent reading can speed up reading as a whole. Silent reading must, of course, be followed by questions to ensure that all the class did read and understand the appropriate section.

Silent reading is often ignored because teachers see reading aloud as a way of teaching pronunciation. This is most unsatisfactory. Teachers must understand that texts should only be read aloud which have been written to be read aloud — poetry, rhymes, and dialogues. Very few prose texts are intended to be read aloud and asking students to do so is to ask them to do something completely unnatural.

If teachers insist on students reading aloud, there are two golden rules — it must be *prepared;* it must be done in a *variety* of ways.

1. At very low levels, the teacher reads, followed by the class reading chorally sentence by sentence.

2. Also for low levels, the class repeats chorally after the tape (more difficult than after the teacher).

3. The teacher reads a paragraph, then the class reads the paragraph chorally, possibly followed by an individual reading the same paragaph.

4. An individual reads sentence by sentence after the teacher.

5. Pupils prepare their parts — the class is divided into groups and each group prepares, for example, a paragraph, then one representative from each group reads so that the whole text is read aloud. In the case of a dialogue, groups prepare different speakers. In all cases the teacher goes from group to group helping with pronunciation, stress and intonation problems quietly, before anybody reads anything for the whole class.

6. With dialogues, students prepare in pairs, the teacher goes round and helps, and then all students read aloud in pairs simultaneously before one pair reads aloud for the whole class.

Texts (in the broad sense, including dialogues) remain one of the main methods of input of new language into the lesson. They are a part of the lesson which can easily drag and, as they so frequently come at the beginning of the lesson, they can create a dead and deadening atmosphere. Varying the method of reading — letting people read in groups, individually, silently, occasionally using **only** the teacher or tape — minimises the possibility of the text killing the lesson.

8. Use short questions during intensive reading

Sometimes you may decide, particularly with a large school class, to read a text yourself. Even this simple technique can, however, be improved by adding simple questions as you read. The purpose of these questions is not to test comprehension, but to ensure that students are following, and to help them maintain concentration. The teacher simply stops at frequent points during the text and poses simple questions, often requiring only a single word or phrase!

> Andy switched on the radio. *(What did he do?)* It was just after 6 o'clock *(What time?)* There was no music. Instead there was a fog warning *(A what?)* Andy slowed down a little. He was just in time. He saw a wall of fog *(What did he see?)* He started to drive much more carefully. *(Much more ...?)*

In this example there are too many questions but the type of question is important — they do not require manipulation of the text, or extended comprehension. They can be answered if the students are following the text and have heard the last two or three words the teacher has read.

These questions are most effective if used on a second reading of a text. They are not appropriate with a text which is particularly difficult, where they will serve to disturb, rather than help, the students' concentration.

A word of warning is necessary. This technique can help to keep a class alert while doing intensive reading. It does not, however, help them to *read* better. Reading involves the reader building up a complex picture of the text, and questions of this type interrupt this process. If, however, the text is primarily intended to introduce new vocabulary or structure into the lesson the technique can be practically useful — particularly on warm afternoons!

9. Don't ask *What does ... mean?* Use definition questions

Many teachers, including native speakers, find explaining new items difficult. It is a skill which students will not need outside the classroom, and something they will find extremely difficult. There is, therefore, no point in asking students *What does . . . mean?* Experience shows that if they are asked this question they normally respond with a simple translation. Providing that is all the teacher expects, the question occasionally has a limited use.

In doing word study, however, the "definition question" is much more valuable — the teacher provides the definition, and invites the student to use a new word:

T   What word in the text meant very very big?
S1   Enormous.
T   Good yes, and what word meant worried and upset?
S2   Anxious.
T   That's right, can we all say that please — anxious.
C   Anxious.

As this short transcript shows, definition questions have two important advantages — the teacher does the difficult work of verbalising a definition, and the students have to locate *and say* the new word or phrase.

The same technique can be used for functional phrases where the teacher asks a question such as:

What phrase does John use when he wants to tell Mary the best thing to do next? (*Why don't you . . .*)?

Definition questions are an important part of the teacher's strategy in following up the presentation of new language in a text, and also from a tape recording.

10. Students cannot use what they cannot say

Textbook units frequently begin with a prose text or a dialogue intended for intensive study. These, by definition, contain new language items. Students cannot use these until they know how to say them. If they have only heard the tape, teacher, or one of their classmates reading the text, many students will still feel inhibited at saying a new item.

Teachers sometimes ask after the text has been read *Is there anything you don't understand?* and, even more foolishly, *Is there anything you can't say?* It is not completely clear how the student is supposed to answer this second question!

The wise teacher, *before* going on to comprehension questions, or other material which exploits the text, does brief choral and individual pronunciation of *all* the items students may find it difficult to say. Using the technique CIP discussed elsewhere (page 67) as many as a dozen items can be practised in this way in a matter of three or four minutes. This time is far from wasted as it increases students' confidence before going on to the principal work of exploiting the new material of the text.

11. "Difficult" words are not the same as long words

Teachers have a tendency, when looking at the "difficult words" after students have read a text, to equate 'difficult words' with 'long words'. *Difficult* does not refer to the intrinsic meaning of the words, but to the difficulty for a particular student or group of students. A word has an appearance, a sound, and a meaning. A word will be "difficult" for students if any one of those factors confuse.

1. If the pronunciation is not reflected by the spelling, teachers should ensure that they give a model pronunciation, and follow with choral and individual repetition.

2. If the word looks similar in the students' own language but is different in meaning, particular attention should be drawn to it. For most European learners the English word *sympathetic* is a difficult word, because they have a word in their own language which *looks* similar, *sounds* similar, but is used differently.

3. If a word looks similar, and has a similar meaning, teachers tend to ignore it; because students can understand it, teachers do not see that it can still be "difficult". An example would be the English word *opera*, and the French word *opéra*.

In examining, explaining, and practising "the difficult words", teachers need to think of each of spelling, pronunciation, and meaning and not concentrate only on the last.

12. 'Correction questions' prompt student language

A response is linked linguistically with the remark which prompted it. Although this is obvious, may teachers fail to recognise it in forming 'questions' to put to students. It is all too easy to question students in such a way that you elicit only a sequence of *Yes* and *No* answers:

T Did Jane arrive early?
S1 Yes.
T Was it raining?
S2 No.

The simplest technique to avoid this is for the teacher to make a wrong statement followed by a question tag, stimulating the student to *both* a formal answer *(No)* and the additional, correct information.

T Jane arrived late, didn't she?
S1 No, she was early.
T The sun was shining, wasn't it?
S2 No, it was raining.

This technique may be applied both to comprehension questions after a text, and as a general conversational technique. It both stimulates more language from the student, and ensures that the language stimulated is more natural.

13. Not all comprehension questions check understanding

Notice what happens with the following text and "comprehension" questions:

The sharve thrang up the hill.

T   What did the sharve do?
S1 Thrang up the hill.
T   Good. Where did it thring?
S2 Up the hill.
T   Good. What thrang up the hill?
S3 The sharve.
T   That's right, and how did it get there?
S4 It thrang.
T   That's right, can you give me the principal parts?
S5 Thring, thrang, thrung.
T   Good. Now, do you think it was tired when it got to the top?
C   ???

It is possible to produce a nonsense text, and ask questions which are all "correctly" answered but none of which exhibit any kind of understanding — how can they when the text itself is nonsense!

The answers do exhibit a certain understanding of basic English structure, such as the fact that the first word of the sentence is probably the subject, but such manipulations do not reveal understanding.

There are three kinds of "comprehension questions":

a. Those where the answer may be *read* directly from the text.

b. Those where the answer is a simple structural manipulation of the grammar of the text.

c. External questions — it is necessary to understand how the words of the text relate to something *outside* the text. In the example it was only the last question which was a genuine comprehension question in this way.

The first kind of question — where the answer can be read — is almost useless save perhaps for checking that students know where you are in the text. The second kind is useful only for intensive language practice — if the teacher wishes students to say a particular word or phrase. To check understanding, it is *only* the third kind of question which is effective.

The easiest way to construct questions of this kind is to ask questions which expect the answer *No;* the question is in some way based on a false assumption. A short example illustrates this:

> *Mr Smith hates getting up early. He loves to stay in bed late. During the week he gets up at 8 o'clock but at weekends he sometimes stays in bed until 10.*

Does Mr Smith like getting up early?
Does he get up at the same time every day?
He gets up at 9 o'clock on Saturdays, doesn't he?

These questions, because they introduce external ideas, do test comprehension. An understanding of *hate,* for example, involves understanding that it is "not liking". An understanding of *weekend,* means identifying it with *Saturday.*

In general, comprehension questions which require the responder to "correct" the questioner, do test comprehension.

14. Use comprehension and conversation questions together

Comprehension questions are about the text; conversation questions about the students. Conversation questions involve the students individually and personally responding to what they are studying. Comprehension questions are related to the immediate common experience of the class — the text — and provide a common basis for development of the lesson.

Comprehension questions used alone make the text remote, and, unless it is of exceptional interest, rather boring. Conversation questions involve individuals, but do not keep the class moving forward *together*. Combined, the lesson develops with everyone involved, and individuals personally involved.

Here is a simple example:

> *When she opened the envelope and read the letter, she found she had won the first prize: £5,000! She wondered whether to spend it or save it.*

What did she find out from the letter?
How do you think she felt? How would **you** feel?
Did she know what to do with it?
What would **you** do with £5,000

15. If you read a dialogue, distinguish the two speakers clearly

If students' books are closed while you are reading a dialogue aloud, they may have difficulty in identifying which character is speaking at a particular time. If you try to help them by varying your voice, you may have to over-exaggerate, sound ridiculous, and distract students from the task.

Instead, help them to visualize the conversation by changing position for each speaker (facing opposite ways) or perhaps by using your hands as puppets and raising a different one for each speaker. This can be amusing and effective if your hands "talk" to each other like this:

Chapter 11

Techniques — Conversation

Mark each of these statements before and after you read the chapter.
Mark each statement
> ✔ if you *agree.*
> X if you *disagree.*
> ? if you are *undecided.*

1. Conversation lessons need detailed preparation.	
2. The best conversation lessons are usually about serious topics.	
3. The teacher should encourage everyone to contribute.	
4. Avoid provocative remarks in conversation classes!	
5. Group work is often a good basis for a conversation lesson.	

Techniques — Conversation

1. Exploit opportunities for short spontaneous conversations

It is usually a mistake to plan a conversation into a lesson. Planned conversations usually degenerate into silence or involve only a small number of students. This is inevitable — if the topic is too general it will not excite interest, if it is too specific some students will be interested, and others not.

Natural conversation outside the classroom is spontaneous. It ebbs and flows, and different people contribute in different ways. Some people are naturally talkative, and others naturally quiet. For these reasons it is unwise to expect similar contributions from all the students in classroom conversation. As far as possible, the features of natural conversation should be incorporated into the classroom activity.

Classroom conversation will be most effective if it arises naturally and spontaneously from the text, an example, a remark made by a student or something which *happens* during the lesson. The noise of a heavy lorry passing the window is more likely to stimulate comment from the class than any discussion which you have decided in advance.

Probably the least successful of all language lessons are so-called "conversation lessons." The reason is obvious — to *require* a group of people to talk about a given topic, for a given length of time, with each person contributing similarly is completely unnatural. From a language teaching point of view it is also very suspect since the skills required to contribute to a real conversation involve the ability to formulate your ideas quickly, to interrupt naturally and in the right place, to agree or disagree pleasantly — often only smiling or nodding. Preparation forms no part of natural conversation. Spontaneity is not a recommendation for classroom conversation, it is essential.

2. Don't flog a dead horse

As soon as you see interest in a particular topic is flagging, drop it immediately even if you, the teacher, find the subject fascinating. The purpose of conversation in a lesson is to give the students a chance to talk about something that interests *them*. In real life if sensitive participants in a conversation realise that a topic is not of interest to the other person, they change the subject. The same applies to the classroom. Your students will think you are a bore if you insist on pumping them for a response when it is obvious that they have nothing more to say.

3. Encourage contributions without interfering

Natural conversation is a relaxed activity; ideally, classroom conversation should be relaxed too. Too often it is inhibiting — the teacher asks questions such as *What do you think, Tomas?* — in fact Tomas may not be thinking about the issue at all and, if he is, may have very little to say about it. He may want to agree with the previous speaker, or he may have a complex and interesting view which he knows he cannot express with his current level of English. Teachers need to remember that, in introducing "conversation" into a lesson, they are introducing one of the most difficult *total* skills of language use — the ability to combine the accurate expression of your ideas with their presentation in a social situation. Students are inhibited by lack of language, and by the fact that this kind of activity normally does not take place in large groups. Teachers should, therefore, expect only simple contributions and be content to encourage these. Encouragement can take the form of a general question, an enquiring look, a smile, and, perhaps most importantly of all, a pause, during which students have time to formulate their thoughts and to decide what they wish to say, and how they wish to say it.

Teachers will not encourage students to talk by pressurising them with questions or by constantly "helping" by finishing students' sentences for them. A pleasant, relaxed atmosphere, and a few moments silence from the teacher are more likely to be effective.

Teachers must be careful, too, not to discourage contributions by jumping on mistakes. Of all classroom activities, "conversation" is the one which most obviously concentrates on fluency rather than accuracy. Accordingly, teachers must *not* correct small structural errors, and, if they are to provide any correction at all, it must come *after* the conversation rather than interrupting its flow.

Language teachers seldom realize how dominant they are in a language classroom; they control drills, exercises and texts; they initiate most activities. This is most unlike real life, so in those parts which most resemble natural situations, you must learn to take a back seat.

4. Conversation does not need to be about serious issues

Conversation outside the classroom is most frequently about very banal topics — a TV programme we have seen, news about a mutual friend, the weather, the fact the bus is late, etc. Only relatively occasionally do we discuss more serious issues.

When many language teachers talk about "a conversation class", they are more likely to have in mind discussions of relatively serious "issues". Many textbooks reflect this concern with "issues" by having chapters on "the role of Women", "Pollution," etc. There is logically no more reason for students to express their views on the role of women in the English lesson than in physics and, bearing in mind that in the English lesson they are required to express their views in a language over which they have an imperfect, and often rather poor, command, it is hardly surprising that some students are positively unwilling to express their views on a subject about which they may not actually care. While textbook writers naturally choose topic areas which they think will interest their readers (itself a dangerous assumption), teachers should beware of "big issues" as the basis of conversation lessons. Many experienced teachers will tell you that it is frequently easier to stimulate comment from a class about less serious topics. Rather surprisingly, it is often easiest of all to stimulate comment about something which is, intrinsically, totally *un*important.

5. Provocative statements are often better than questions

We have already noted that it is often better to make a 'wrong' tagged statement rather than ask a question if the student is to be stimulated to produce language in, for example, the follow-up to a text. The same technique applies to stimulating a student response in free activities. Normal conversational discussion does not usually consist of a string of questions and answers; the speakers respond to each other's attitudes and opinions. Students can often be much more willing to respond to a provocative statement than to a question. Not *Do you think boys and girls should go to the same schools?*, but *I think it's better for boys and girls to be in different classes.*

Teachers are sometimes inhibited about expressing their own views in this provocative way. Such worries are not usually well-founded, as students half realise that the teacher is provoking them, and half expect their teacher to hold unusual views anyway!

If teachers do feel inhibited, however, they can overcome the difficulty by introducing a "friend" into the lesson — *An English friend of mine told me/ wrote to me the other day that he thought it was better that . . . .* Needless to say, the "friend" can be given any views which the teacher finds convenient!

6. Problem solving is often an excellent basis for "conversation"

Most teachers now recognise the importance of "the information gap" in lanlanguage teaching. In normal life we do not speak unless we have a reason to do so. The most common reason is the existence of an information gap — the two speakers have different sets of information (in the broad sense) and the conversation consists of the exchange of information. Many situational or pair work practices are now based on this principle.

It can, however, be even more effective if more fully developed. Teachers can, for example, deliberately divide the class into two groups, have the students collect different sets of information — perhaps information from reference books about a topic they are studying. When the two groups return to report what they have found, each has a natural interest in what the other has to say and, if some part of the information is unclear or incomplete, it is natural to ask for clarification or further information. It is also natural, for example, to express surprise about certain bits of information found by the other students. Such natural involvement is closer to normal language use outside the classroom than any contrived classroom discussion.

In a similar way, problem solving of all kinds creates information gaps, and, therefore, the conditions for natural language use. Such problem solving activities have a further, and extremely important, advantage — namely, they invite the students to use information from experience outside the language learning classroom. A simple example may illustrate the point. On numerous occasions we have invited students to pick "the odd man out" from the following:

apple pear tomato banana peach

On every single occasion at least one member of the group questioned has suggested *tomato* and, when asked why, has replied *It's the only one which isn't a fruit.* The remarkable thing is that, on every single occasion with no further prompting, another member of the group has immediately responded *Oh, but it is.*

The "problem" is hardly important; several "correct" answers are possible — why not *banana* because it's the only one which is yellow — but the extraordinary thing is that students *spontaneously* respond to each other's opinions and ideas. Such responses are not, however, accidental — they are based on the fact that students bring into the classroom knowledge which they can use. They do not feel at risk in discussing such a trivial problem; it is within their linguistic capability; different people can, legitimately, have different opinions; people care *enough* to "correct" others' opinions, but not enough to feel inhibited by the topic.

Problem solving activities may range from simple puzzles of the kind just mentioned to the kind of full-scale management training problems sometimes used to teach business students. They may take anything from two or three minutes to several hours of classroom time. The essential feature is, however, always the same — by generating a natural information gap they ensure that language use is a spontaneous, natural activity, vastly more involving and more helpful for students than the contrived set-piece discussions frequently planned by teachers as "conversation classes".

7. Encourage active listening

Unfortunately, the normal pattern of classroom conversations is teacher-question, student-answer. Natural conversation does not, however, consist of strings of questions and answers; frequently when one speaker makes a statement, the other person signals interest and encourages the first to expand. When one speaker delivers a relatively long monologue, the listeners constantly signal their reactions. Reflect this in the conversations you have in your classroom. At all levels, teach the kind of responses which encourage the speaker to expand:

Really?
That's very interesting.
Were you? Did you? Has she? i.e. (auxiliary verb) (pronoun)

You yourself, while conducting the conversation part of the lesson, will find that if *you* use such tactics, the students will automatically respond and expand. If you have taught them in advance, you will find that they will start using them too. Aim to stop them relying on direct questions which can so easily make them seem as if they are interrogating the listener.

Chapter 12

Some misunderstood language points

Mark each of these statements before and after you read the chapter.
Mark each statement
         ✔ if you *agree.*
         X if you *disagree.*
         ? if you are *undecided.*

1. *Some* does not occur in negative sentences.	
2. The present simple refers to the future as *fact.*	
3. English continuous forms refer to *periods.*	
4. The *past* participle is used to make the *present* perfect.	
5. Uncountable nouns are singular.	
6. *Could* is the past tense of *can.*	
7. *Must* is stronger than *have to.*	
8. *It's a lovely day, isn't it* is a question.	
9. Stressing an auxiliary can change the meaning of a sentence.	
10. *(Do)* as an auxiliary is an irregularity in English.	

Some Misunderstood Language Points

Early in this book we observed that good rules can help students and, later, that a "rule" was a combination of example, explanation and the relationship between these two. Unfortunately, it often remains true that the element of language teaching which is based on understanding the underlying structure of the language is either avoided by teachers, or handled by them in a way which intimidates and confuses students. Careless, lazy, and off-hand explanations confuse instead of helping. Many textbooks present examples but not explanations, and grammar books sometimes only confuse.

This book is about practical teaching techniques. It is not a grammar book. In this chapter, however, we turn our attention to ten features of English which are frequently badly-taught and even misunderstood by teachers themselves. The examples chosen here are in no sense comprehensive. They are chosen because each exemplifies a general principle which distinguishes good language teaching from bad.

The explanations offered are necessarily brief. The points are much more exhaustively discussed in *The Basic Structure of the English Verb (Michael Lewis, Language Teaching Publications,1985).*

1. some/any

Language teachers often present the "rule":

Some in **positive** sentences
Any in **negatives** and **questions**

despite the fact that they know that all of the following are possible English sentences:

> I like some pop music.
> I like any pop music.
> I don't like some pop music.
> I don't like any pop music.

Teachers, and even books, go to great lengths to explain "special" uses of *some* and *any* in an attempt to preserve the "basic rule" which they have already taught. In fact this rule is completely wrong.

The use of *some* and *any* is determined by *meaning,* not by structure:

Some and **any** are both used for indefinite quantities.
Some is used if the quantity is **restricted** in some way.
Any is used if the quantity is **not restricted.**

This rule, although more abstract and "difficult", covers all uses of *some* and *any,* and their compounds (*somebody, anything,* etc.).

    Some always refers to *part; any* refers to *all* or *none.* The four sentences above may be shown diagrammatically:

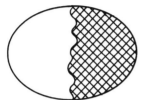

I like some pop music.

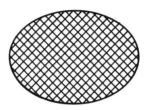

I like any pop music.

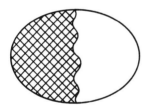

I don't like some pop music.

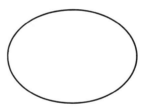

I don't like any pop music.

If **part** of the area is shaded, **some** is used.
If the **whole** area is the same (shaded or unshaded), **any** is used.

    Traditional teaching, ignoring this basic rule, first taught the 'rule' relating to positives, negatives and questions, and then followed with "exceptions" concerning "polite requests" (*Can I get you something to eat?*), anticipated answers (*Have you got some tomatoes, please?*) etc.

    The principle is that if you present a "rule" and then find that you have to present a long string of special cases or exceptions, you should go back to the original rule and question that. On some occasions it may be better to present a fuller, more accurate rule initially, rather than have to deal with a string of 'special cases' which most simplified rules produce.

2. "The Future"

English does not possess a single verb form which is strongly associated with the expression of future time. Several verb forms may be used to talk about the future. Among the most important are:

1. The present simple

My birthday is on Wednesday next week.
We take off at 10 o'clock tomorrow morning.

This form is mostly used if the speaker sees the future as a *fact*, often determined by the calendar or an official timetable.

2. The present continuous

I'm playing tennis with Bill on Saturday.
We're going to Italy for our holidays this year.

This form is usually used when an arrangement has *already* been made. In the speaker's mind there is some event *before* the moment of speaking, which is linked with the future event. In this sense the event "surrounds the moment of speaking" in the same way as with other uses of the present continuous such as *It's raining.*

3. (be) going to

Look at those clouds, it's going to rain.
Oh dear, I'm think I'm going to sneeze.
We're going to move as soon as we can.

This form is usually used when there is some *evidence at the moment of speaking* which leads the speaker to expect the future event. The evidence may be external (clouds, the tickle in the nose) or internal (a decision).

4. The 'll future

Hang on, I'll just get my coat.
Who else'll be there?

This form gives the speaker's opinion (or asks for the listener's opinion) *formed at the moment of speaking*. It refers to future time but is the form which is most closely associated with the speaker's (or listener's) *present opinion*.

The meaning of the individual words of a sentence may mean that particular collocations are impossible (**I'm going to sneeze tomorrow*) or that one form is common and another uncommon. In other cases, the whole group of contrasting sentences, all natural, may be formed:

> *We leave tomorrow.*
> *We are leaving tomorrow.*
> *We're going to leave tomorrow.*
> *We'll leave tomorrow.*

Several points are important — if the students' own language possesses a single form ("the future") strongly associated with the expression of future time, the difference between the various uses in English will be difficult. It will not be sufficient to present each form separately; it will also be necessary to present the forms contrastively, and, rather than simply expecting students to understand the difference, it will be necessary to explore the difference on successive occasions as the students build up a series of pictures of the different uses.

Trying to "simplify" will often confuse, and trying to isolate particular uses will delay, not solve, the problem.

Two important principles emerge from this example — languages are different, often in fundamental ways, and those differences need to be explored, not ignored, if students are to develop a real understanding of, and ability to use, the target language. Secondly, language learning is cyclical. No student could learn one use, then another, then another, without also needing to revise, see contrastively, and constantly look again at the same problems from different points of view.

3. Continuous forms

Any English verb form may occur in either the simple or the continuous. The continuous forms are characterised by containing (*be*) + . . . *ing*.

Simple	Continuous
I live in Birmingham.	I'm living in Birmingham.
They are made in Hong Kong.	They're being made in Hong Kong.
I've waited three months.	I've been waiting three months.
I'll see him tomorrow.	I'll be seeing him tomorrow.

All continuous forms are used if the speaker (writer), at the moment of use, sees the event described as going on for a *limited period* of time. Both elements of that definition are important — the speaker conceptualises the event as a *period*; the speaker also conceptualises the period as *limited*. It is not a question of objective fact, but of the speaker's subjective interpretation of the situation at the moment of language use.

Again, two important principles emerge — teachers must always be aware of the fact that in learning a new language students are sometimes learning new concepts, not simply new words for old things. Understanding is necessary, and this takes time. Secondly, most textbooks present the present continuous, and perhaps contrast it with the present simple. They present the past continuous, perhaps contrasted with the past simple. Rarely do they gather together the continuous forms and show that they have something *in common*. For the more advanced student, it helps to consider together points of *similarity*, as well as points of contrast.

Most importantly of all, continuous forms are a feature of *English*, but not of most European languages. If the teacher is constantly contrasting English and the students' native language — perhaps using a method which refers frequently to translation — students will become more and more confused. The more the study of English is based on contrasting English with English, rather than English with the student's native language, the more likely students are to understand how English is used. This does not mean explanations and discussion of language problems may not take place in the student's native language, but that it should be based on problems of contrast within English.

4. go — went — gone

English is not a highly inflected language. Most verbs have only four forms:

walk — walks — walked — walking

Some irregular verbs have five:

go — goes — went — gone — going

Even the verb **(be)** has only eight forms.

With so few forms, it should not be necessary to have a complex system of names for the forms. Terminology should always aim at being both accurate and helpful. Many of the traditional grammatical names are certainly not helpful when used to describe English verb forms. The "past participle", is used to make the *present* perfect, and all passives (*made; I've made a mistake; They're made of wood*). Students must often wonder what has happened — why is the *past* participle, used for the *present* perfect?

A much simpler system of terminology is possible. What is wrong with these simple names?

Goes — *The —s form*
Going — *The —ing form*
Go — *The first form*
Went — *The second form*
Gone — *The third form*

Many students learn the irregular verb lists, using as a pattern *go — went — gone,* so that the terms *first, second, third* are helpful. Their main advantage is that they are *not* confusing.

Using this very simple set of terms it is interesting to note that it is not necessary to use "imperative", "infinitive", "participle", or "gerund", which are all terms which confuse students and make the task of learning the foreign language seem more difficult.

The principle is simple — terminology should describe, and be as helpful as possible. Teachers should introduce terminology only if they are sure students understand it, and it is necessary. Much conventional terminology, while suitable for more highly inflected languages, is quite unsuitable for English and makes the student's task unnecessarily complicated.

5. Countable and uncountable nouns

Like verbs, English nouns hardly change except to form plurals (usually by the addition of —s). Even so, students often find them confusing because they are not presented clearly with the one important contrast for English nouns. English nouns divide into two groups — *countable* and *uncountable.*

Countable nouns are nouns which are conceptualised in units. Because they are conceptualised in units they can collocate with numbers, are preceded by *a/an,* and followed by either singular or plural verbs as appropriate.

Uncountable nouns are *not* conceptualised in units; they are *never* preceded by numbers, nor by *a/an.* They are always followed by a singular verb but, and this is the important point, they are *not* singular.

Teachers who use the terms "singular" and "uncountable" interchangeably are going to confuse students.

The difference between countable and uncountable nouns is based on one difficult idea, namely that a language can divide words not according to meaning, or structure, but arbitrarily, into grammatical groups. Many English students when first meeting, for example, French would like to know *why* some nouns are "masculine" and others "feminine". There is no answer — French divides nouns into two groups, two grammatical categories. When students learn a new noun they need to know which group it belongs to. For many students this is a difficult idea — they would like to be given an explanation or rule which tells them which group a noun will belong to.

The distinction in English between countable and uncountable nouns is a *grammatical* distinction of this kind. Some general hints can be given — concrete objects which can be counted are countable (*boy, chair, tree*), but abstract nouns can also be countable (*idea, worry*). Words which are similar in meaning may belong to different categories - *weather* is uncountable, but *climate* is countable. Several words which are commonly plural in European languages are uncountable in English (*information, furniture*).

It is important to recognise that nouns cannot be sorted decisively into countable and uncountable. It is not the noun, but a particular use of the noun, which is either countable or uncountable:

I've been there many times.	Countable
Time flies.	Uncountable
She has lovely hair.	Uncountable
There's a hair on your jacket.	Countable
Wars have never solved problems.	Countable
War has never solved problems.	Uncountable
This room needs some colour.	Uncountable
This room needs some bright colours.	Countable

This is a difficult idea. Words cannot be sorted by their form, only by their meaning. Teachers must be prepared to discuss this with classes, and to return to the discussion from time to time as examples arise.

The principle is that students must be introduced carefully to the idea of grammatical categories, and it must be made clear to them that they must not expect those categories to be reflected by the categories they are used to in their own language.

Secondly, having introduced the terms — in this case *countable, uncountable, singular* and *plural* — teachers must be careful and consistent in the way they use them.

6. can/could

At first sight each of these forms has many different uses:

Can I have an apple?	**Could I have an apple?**
Can you travel anywhere you like?	**Could you travel anywhere you like?**
Can you drive?	**Could you drive?**

Many teachers would explain that the first pair of sentences was similar in meaning but "*could* is more polite than *can*", but it is impossible to apply that explanation to the third pair of sentences.

The basic confusion arises by thinking of *could* as "the past tense" of *can*. It may appear so in the contrast:

> *Sorry I can't come on Saturday.*
> *Sorry I couldn't come last Saturday.*

but clearly there is no connection with past time in:

> *Can you lend me a pound?*
> *Could you lend me a pound?*

As with the *some/any* examples already discussed, it is essential to question the basic explanation.

Perhaps surprisingly it is easy to find an explanation which covers *all* uses of *can* and *could* consistently: *Could* is always *more remote* than *can*, although that "remoteness" may be of different kinds:

> *I could speak better Spanish when I was at school.* (remote in time)
> *You could do it if you tried.* (more remote possibility)
> *Could you lend me a pound please?* (remote in relationship = "more polite").

This example shows an important principle — while it may be a good idea, or even essential, to teach individual uses of a particular form one by one, it is also important to show students that language is not random, but it is based on patterns and that the patterns are consistent. By collecting different uses of *can* and *could* at a suitable stage in the students' learning, and showing that the contrast between them is consistent — *could* is **always** more *remote* than *can* — students are reassured that the task they are undertaking in learning a foreign language is not impossible. The point is also made for them that the most important part of language is *meaning*. Language is not a collection of words and structures, it is a *system* for communicating *meaning*.

7. must/have to

The fundamental difference between *must* and *have to* is that *have to* is used if the speaker is invoking an authority outside himself, while *must* is used if the speaker is the source of the authority.

Sometimes two sentences can appear similar in meaning:

> *I have to catch the 8 o'clock train.*
> *I must catch the 8 o'clock train.*

This is particularly the case if the subject of the sentence is 'I', when the difference between the speaker's understanding of necessity, and the speaker imposing authority on him- or herself is very small.

The difference is more obvious with other subjects:

> *You have to be there by 3 o'clock.*
> *You must be there by 3 o'clock.*

Most foreign learners over-use *must*, and some do not use *have to* at all. The first reason for this is that some European languages possess a word similar in sound and associated in meaning to *must*. There is a second difficulty, however, which is that teachers tend to give personal examples which begin with 'I', where the difference between *must* and *have to* is at its smallest.

If a wide range of examples is chosen, it is much easier to see that the fundamental difference is that both forms refer to *necessity,* but *have to* refers to the speaker's perception of *objective* necessity, while *must* refers to the speaker's *imposition* of *subjective* necessity.

The point is, perhaps, intrinsically difficult. It will not feature in elementary language courses. It does, however, demonstrate a most important principle, namely that the examples must not be chosen to fit a pre-conceived rule, but, if the language is truly to be explored and presented to students, a wide range of examples must be used.

8. Tags

Tags are a very important feature of spoken English. There are many kinds and most textbooks give them only superficial treatment. It is of particular importance to note these four sentences:

She's French — giving information.

Is she French? — asking for information.

She's French, isn't she? — a confirmation tag (see below).

She's French isn't she. — an invitation tag (see below).

Even the most traditional language teaching has identified statements and questions, though it has not usually thought it necessary to describe what they are doing (giving and seeking information). Most reference books, however, identify only one kind of tag, frequently referred to as "question tags". The implication, though not stated, is that they have the same function as questions — they are asking for information. This is not the case. Certain well-known reference books suggest that there are two kinds of tag, said with falling and rising intonation, indicating that the speaker expects either agreement, or confirmation. This too is incorrect and confusing.

The truth is that, said in a certain way, a tagged remark seeks confirmation. Appropriate responses will be:

Yes, that's right.

No, as a matter of fact she isn't/it wasn't/we can't.

Most frequently, however, tags are proposing a direction for the extension of a conversation, inviting the other speaker to develop the conversation. It is clear that the best known example: *It's a lovely day, isn't it* could not be a question — both speakers are obviously well aware of the state of the weather!

What is happening here is that one speaker is inviting the other to make a comment about the weather — not merely to agree, but to offer some new contribution to the conversation. The sentence has little denotative meaning, but an important social function. The student who treats several consecutive invitation tags as questions will be thought socially rather strange:

A You play tennis, don't you.

B Yes.

A You've brought your things with you, haven't you.

B Yes.

A It's a nice day for a game, isn't it.

B Yes.

Tags are extremely important in natural colloquial conversation in English. They are, however, given relatively little treatment in textbooks, or even standard student grammars. Such treatment as is given, is frequently either wrong or confusing. Why?

Two important principles emerge. Tags are hardly ever written (except in private letters), and have been given too little importance in traditional language teaching which was largely based on the written language. Secondly, because the two tags mentioned above — confirmation and invitation tags — are *structurally* identical, teachers, and even textbooks, have tended to treat them as identical. Even modern so-called functional textbooks have made this mistake, although the function of the two sentences is quite different. The principle the teacher needs to bear in mind in looking for an explanation to offer a class is to ask *two* questions — *What* was said? (structure), and *Why* was it said? (function). An understanding of meaning implies an understanding of both structure and function. Knowledge of structures alone is not a knowledge of a language.

9. Auxiliaries

Auxiliaries are of great structural importance in English. They are used in a number of important ways, including the following:

1. Making a negative
n't is added to the end of the first auxiliary.

He can swim	→He **can't** swim
They have gone	→They **haven't** gone

2. Forming questions
Change the order of the subject and the first auxiliary.

He can swim	→**Can he** swim?
They have gone	→**Have they** gone?

3. Making confirmation or invitation tags
Positive sentence/negative tag, negative sentence/positive tag.
Use the first auxiliary.

He can swim.	→He can swim, **can't he.**
She must've gone.	→She must've gone, **mustn't she.**

4. Making surprise or annoyance tags
Positive sentence/positive tag, negative sentence/negative tag.
Use the first auxiliary.

You've met before.	→Oh, you've met before, **have you!**
So you can't come.	→So you can't come, **can't you!**

5. Making an interested response
Use the first auxiliary in what the first speaker says.

A I've been there before.		**A** I'd be surprised.
B **Have** you?		**B** **Would** you?

6. Making a short answer

A Have you been there before?	**A** Can you speak French?
B Yes I **have.**	**B** Yes I **can.**

A I can't understand it.	**A** I was going to tell her.
B No, neither **can** I.	**B** Yes, so **was** I.

7. Emphasis

Pronounce the auxiliary with its full, stressed, form.

They're waiting. They **are** waiting.
He's French. He **is** French.

The last example is of particular importance. It shows clearly that in the spoken language stress contributes as much to meaning as structure; stress is part of the grammar of the language.

Several other principles are illustrated by the importance of the auxiliary. The ability to produce agreement or interested responses, for example, depends on the student's ability to identify automatically the auxiliary which is required. It is an example of language as habit, and reminds the teacher of the importance of intensive oral practice.

The similarity of, for example, agreement responses:

Have you ... Can you ... Did you ...
→ Yes I have. → Yes I can. → Yes I did.

I can't ... I haven't ... I didn't ...
→ No neither can I. → No neither have I. → No neither did I.

emphasises the importance for the teacher of drawing the student's attention to similarities as well as differences. If students are to acquire the ability to generate language quickly and accurately, they need both intensive practice, and an ability to see the patterns.

10. (Do) as the dummy auxiliary

This is the feature of English structure which is probably most misunderstood. Very often questions and negatives made with (**do**) (*do, does, did*) are treated as exceptions. In fact, English possesses totally consistent patterns and there is one rule of English which is helpful for students and teachers which occurs in far too few textbooks. It may be stated as follows:

> If a particular pattern is made using an auxiliary and you want to use that pattern with a sentence which does not contain an auxiliary, you follow the usual pattern and use (**do**) (*do, does, did*) as the dummy auxiliary. The patterns are always formed in exactly the same way.

The examples under *Auxiliaries* above, show the patterns clearly:

1. Negatives

He can swim. → He can't swim.

He goes often. He went yesterday.
→ *He does go often.* → *He did go yesterday.*
→ He **doesn't** go often. → He **didn't** go yesterday.

2. Making questions

He can swim. → Can he swim?

He goes often. He went yesterday.
→ *He does go often.* → *He did go yesterday.*
→ **Does** he go often? → **Did** he go yesterday?

3. Making confirmation or invitation tags

He can swim. → He can swim, can't he.

He knows her. → He knows her, **doesn't** he.
They went. → They went, **didn't** they.

4. Making a surprise or annoyance tag

You've met before. → You've met before, have you!

You know each other. → You know each other, **do** you!

5. Making an interested response

A I've been there before. **A** I'd be very surprised.
B Have you? **B** Would you?

A I know them well. **A** I saw them yesterday.
B **Do** you? **B** **Did** you?

6. Making a short answer

A Have you been there before? **A** Can you speak French?
B Yes I have. **B** Yes I can.
　　No I haven't. 　　No I can't.

A Do you know where it is? **A** Did you post that letter?
B Yes I **do.** **B** Yes I **did.**
　　No I **don**'t. 　　No I **did**n't.

A I can come on Saturday. **A** I was going to tell her.
B Yes, so can I. **B** Yes, so was I.

A I enjoyed that. **A** He doesn't like it.
B Yes, so **did** I. **B** No, neither **do** I.

7. Emphasis

They're waiting. They are waiting.
I feel you should ask him. I **do** feel you should ask him.
I waited an hour. I **did** wait an hour.

This very powerful rule — the use of (**do**) as the dummy auxiliary — is of considerable importance and makes clear one of the most important principles of good language teaching — that whenever there is a pattern which helps to reduce the memory load for the student, the teacher should draw attention to that pattern. Too often, teachers emphasise difficulties and differences and ignore opportunities to systematise and simplify.

Further reading

More about language teaching

The Lexical Approach, Michael Lewis, 0 906717 99 X
An evaluation of the theory and practice of ELT with a clear statement of a new direction. The Lexical Approach develops current thinking by invalidating the grammar / vocabulary distinction and placing lexis in all its forms at the centre of language presentation and practice.

Implementing the Lexical Approach, Michael Lewis, 1 899396 60 8
Develops the theoretical position set out in The Lexical Approach, adds new insights and gives comprehensive suggestions to enable teachers to take the approach directly into the classroom.

The English Verb, Michael Lewis, 0 906717 40 X
A step-by-step survey of the central problem of English – the structure of the verb. Extensive discussion of the grammar itself, and of classroom rules. Practical hints on how to present grammar in the classroom. Recommended reading on many courses.

A Teachers' Grammar, R.A. Close, 0 906717 48 5
Introduces the basic concepts of English grammar to teachers. It should be read by all teachers before they start explaining grammar in the classroom. Most grammar books list a mass of details. Close argues that the grammar of English is a matter of relatively few, but very powerful, distinctions.

Business English

One to One, Peter Wilberg, 0 906717 61 2
Despite its title, this book provides a general introduction to the teaching of business English. It provides background information, discussion of theoretical issues, and contains hundreds of practical suggestions for what to do in this type of class. For anyone who teaches business English, this book is a must-have.

Teaching Children

**Teaching English to Children, Wendy Scott and Lisbeth Ytreberg,
0 582 74606 X**
A highly practical introduction to the world of young learners. An excellent resource book and full of practical ideas for lessons and activities.

Teaching Examination Classes

Exam Classes, Peter May, 0 19 437208 1
Contains information about all the main British, European, and American examination boards as well as lots of practical activities to use in exam classes.

For reference

Grammar Reference

Practical English Usage, Michael Swan, 0 19 431197 X
The organisation of this book makes it easy to use, and the author's straight-forward style means that his tremendous knowledge and understanding of English grammar is made accessible to readers who have little or no background in the subject. It is equally useful to teachers and to students.

Dictionaries

The four main ELT dictionaries are:

Oxford Advanced Learner's Dictionary
Cobuild English Dictionary
Longman Dictionary of Contemporary English
Cambridge International Dictionary of English

All these dictionaries are excellent. A dictionary designed for native speakers, but potentially of great use to EFL teachers and advanced learners is the **Collins Concise Dictionary and Thesaurus, 0 00 470844 X.**

The LTP Dictionary of Selected Collocations, 1 899396 55 1
A new kind of dictionary for teachers and learners which lists collocations rather than meanings. Conventional dictionaries are limited in the amount of information they can give on collocation. This dictionary gives 50,000 collocations of 2,000 essential nouns and 5,000 adverbs with over 1,200 verbs and adjectives. DOSC is essential for students who have to write essays or reports, anyone involved in translation, and has an active classroom use for all students at intermediate level and above.